GW00401077

Inspired Selling

Inspired Selling

A BOOK OF IDEAS OPPORTUNITIES AND RENEWAL

J T AUER

KOGAN PAGE

First published in Canada in French (*La Joie de Vendre*) and English, entitled *The Joy of Selling*, by Stoddart Publishing Co Ltd, 34 Lesmill Road, Toronto, Canada M3B 2T6.

This edition first published in Great Britain in 1991 by Kogan Page Ltd, 120 Pentonville Road, London N1 9JN.

British Library Cataloguing in Publication Data

A CIP record for this book is available from the British Library.

ISBN 0–7494–0485–X

Printed and bound in Great Britain by Biddles Ltd, Guildford

To my wife Madeleine, without whose love, dedication, fairness, understanding and professionalism this book would never have been written.

Contents

Part 4: Sell! Do Not Offer

Part 5: Closing the Sale Means Asking for the Cheque

Part 1

Let Us Be Proud of the Selling Profession

Chapter 1

Selling: A 'Dirty' Word?

Before deciding to give up my engineering career, I must admit I hesitated a lot. Even to this day, some of my close friends and relatives do not understand my reasons for changing jobs. Often people asked me, 'What made you decide to change your life so radically?' Answering honestly, I have always stated that in the early stages, my only motivating factor was money. I wanted to earn more.

The year I switched careers, my supervisor, the one who introduced me to my new career, kept showing me the commission cheques he was receiving in the post from head office. My friend's earnings seemed enormous. I asked myself, 'What have I got to lose? Why not try? If I don't succeed, I can always go back to my engineering career.' This whole thinking process took time, a great deal of time, for I saw many barriers to entering the sales profession. During my travels I often saw signs that said 'No Soliciting' or 'Salesmen, Use the Service Entrance'. Change came slowly, North America progressing a bit faster than Europe. Today, the selling profession has become a recognised and rewarding career.

At a later stage, in Europe, when I started teaching and giving seminars, the big handicap I encountered was the lack of recognition for salespeople. I found that the words *selling* and *salespeople* were not respected, and in many countries our profession was looked down upon.

But all this is changing. Allow me to say it loud and clear: 'Ladies and Gentlemen, *congratulations*, you and I have been able to vanquish, conquer and defeat all preconceptions and antiquated notions about the selling profession. We are members of an élite group and can be proud to be working in the noblest and most interesting profession in the world: that of the salesperson.'

It is shameful that, around the world, many of our professional colleagues are still hiding behind invented titles and names such as representative, consultant, broker, assistant, marketing expert, manager, solicitor, retailer, promotion executive, wholesaler, agent, dealer, delegate. Most of them still hesitate to admit openly that we are all *salespeople*.

May I ask you to follow my lead and try to show the world that our business activity is a pleasant and pleasing one! Don't be shy! Admit it! Tell everyone that our profession gives us the opportunity to help others. A doctor brings a cure to the ill, a dentist helps people in pain, a lawyer helps those in trouble, but we, the salespeople, can bring comfort and render service to all.

Salespeople are proud people

All successful salespeople think proudly of their achievements. Most of them are not vain – they are not afraid to look to friends for opinions and advice – but their self-confidence helps them to overcome most difficulties. They are proud of their reputations. Although some are too proud to admit or discuss failure (mainly when things don't go their way), they accept their mistakes and come back smiling, ready to do battle. They seldom complain and rarely cry. Their pride is too strong.

Some people I have met have a tendency to condemn pride. They do this only because they confuse pride with arrogance, conceit or vanity. We need to remember that most famous people in history have been proud people. Their pride has pushed them on to ever greater achievements, and some of them have even been 'proud' of their modesty. Others have been vain about their self-effacement, but this is not pride. Most proud people who have achieved great things don't brag about their exceptional qualities, but they will tell you readily that they got on the bus as it was going past.

Like all good athletes, most of us are fighters, determined to win. We enjoy being admired for our victories. We like to recount our successes. We will fight so that we don't lose. We like nothing better than an uninterrupted string of achievements. In order to improve yourself and avoid the influence of negative thoughts that might be transmitted by close friends or family members, may I suggest that you look around you and observe a successful salesperson. Try to get to know someone who you know only by reputation. You will discover that many of them are as proud of themselves and their successes as I have just described. Follow their example, follow their lead, do as they do.

After you close a sale, feel good! If you are satisfied with yourself, don't be shy about it. Tell the world! Be proud of your success! Don't rest; try to close another sale immediately.

One of my best salespeople enjoyed telling one and all: 'The next best thing to sex is leaving a client's home with a signed cheque.' Can you believe that? I do! Salespeople are proud people. Be proud too!

Summary

1. Selling is one of the most enjoyable professions in the world.
2. Be proud of your profession as a salesperson.
3. Salespeople are fighters. Follow their lead. Imitate the salespeople you admire.
4. Be happy after closing a big sale. Share your happiness with others. Don't stop. Keep selling!

Chapter 2

Why Choose the Selling Profession?

In short order, my new sales career gave me a hefty increase in earnings. Having reached my primary goal, I felt good about my decision.

When I joined the sales force, I was told that 'only commission' was being paid. I wondered how I would be able to make a living, not knowing what my monthly cheque would amount to. This early trauma made it difficult for me to adjust. However, my supervisor explained simply: 'My corporation pays commission only because our salespeople want to earn as much as they feel they are worth. They reject all restrictions. If they work hard and are successful, they could earn as much as ten times their previous salary.' From then on, it was easy to understand that selling for commission only allowed professionals to earn a lot of money. This method of payment brought daily stimulation to expert salespeople as well as trainees. Since then, I have never considered a salaried position.

After starting to recruit trainees myself, I made a strange and interesting discovery: it can be dangerous and troublesome to certain people to earn large amounts of money early in their careers. If you fail to show newcomers that in our profession perseverance is a must, they have a tendency to let go or take it easy after a good month. Often, salespeople will feel that after closing a sale they have earned enough money for the next two or three months. They should never forget, however, to continue working steadily. If they make the mistake of stopping altogether, they will need five times as much energy and willpower to start again.

Once I had achieved my goal of financial independence, new satisfactions came to light. I suddenly discovered a new world, and met many interesting people. At first it was a shock. I began to offer my services to everyone from building workers to engineers to bank executives. Luckily, I made new friends and I felt good with most of them. My new career gave me joy day after day and, along with that, all kinds of freedom. I had the freedom to work on *what* I wanted to do, to talk and sell to *anybody*; the freedom to work *where I wanted*; and, finally, the freedom to work *when I wanted*. These, as far as I am concerned, are the true liberties in life. They allowed me to stay at home with my family at any time, but also gave me opportunities to travel and sell in foreign countries whenever I felt like it.

My discoveries did not stop there: suddenly the prospect of true security came to light. This concept became my personal key to success. Think: if you are a free person but do not have financial independence, your freedom is restricted; there are a number of things you are restricted from doing. The same holds true for financial security without freedom. You can be free only when you are doing *what* you want, with *whom* you want and *when* and *where* you want. This independence is one of the greatest advantages of being a professional salesperson.

Another satisfaction of the selling profession is that of rendering service to another person. Trainees do not often think of this benefit, and personally, I did not become aware of it until someone pointed it out to me. In my early selling days, I met a former competitor in the electrical engineering business who told me, 'A personal friend was thrilled the other day to explain how you helped his family with your investment schemes. I had no idea that you represented a financial group. I would be very interested in knowing what you do.' I immediately made an appointment for the next evening.

After giving my presentation, I was surprised to hear my ex-colleague say, 'I am really upset that you did not come to see us earlier. It's a shame to think that we have wasted a whole year not knowing the ins and outs of these savings schemes.' That day I learned how much I could be of service to everyone. From then on, I never hesitated to talk to anyone about the services I was selling.

Summary

1. The selling profession will give you financial independence.
2. Selling gives you the freedom:
   - to work at *what* you want to do
   - to work with *whom* you want to
   - to work *when* and *where* you want to.
3. The freedom of the selling profession gives you true security: the security you give yourself.
4. Selling allows you to be helpful to others.

Chapter 3

The Science of Selling

You probably raised your eyebrows to see selling described as a science. Webster's dictionary defines 'science' as 'systematised knowledge derived from observation, study and experimentation carried on in order to determine the nature or principles of what is being studied'. Why would I call selling a science? Because it embodies complex problems that can be solved only by following exact principles. Just like a doctor who must come up with a diagnosis and later a cure for the patient, the salesperson must learn and apply the basic principles and know-how of selling to each new situation as it is encountered.

Some have even had the audacity to compare the salesperson to a surgeon. If a surgeon fails to remember the basics of the surgical procedures he or she is performing, the chances of the patient recovering are slim. If a salesperson breaks the basic rules of selling, the potential client is unlikely to be receptive to that salesperson again. The basic rules of selling will be covered in Parts 2, 3, 4 and 5 of this book.

Before you play any sport, I am sure you would try to find out the rules of the game. The same goes for selling. Most of the big and interesting sales you have heard about have been closed by professionals who knew and followed the basic rules.

Once you know the rules, you have to practise. If you don't practise a sport, you soon lose your skill: the same applies to selling. When I started, there were few training resources available. I had to rely on my supervisors, on a few books that were difficult to understand and assimilate, and on trial and error. In other words, I learned from my mistakes. As you are starting out today, you have many more resources at hand. You will be able to take courses and seminars, read books and listen to cassettes on the subject. And you can use videotapes to improve your technique. When I started, video was not as prevalent as it is now, so I trained in front of a mirror. That was my way of learning to talk, convince, demonstrate and emphasise.

Read and study everything you can about the product you are selling. You must know the product fully before you can convince someone else to buy it. Answers to technical questions must come to you quickly and without hesitation. Knowing the product will also help you to prepare a useful presentation. It should be made at your own speed, in your own words. Of course, you can always use someone else's text, but please do not forget to adapt it to your own style.

When you read, ask yourself, 'How can I use this concept? How can I take advantage of this idea?' All salespeople lose sales. No one has ever sold to every prospect! Even the very best cannot perform the feat of selling to everyone they meet. But intensive study of your own product and that of your competitors will help you to lose fewer prospective clients. Expert understanding of your market, corporations, competitors, delivery schedules, prices and all other factors of your service or product will make it easier to avoid losing an order. And the more you know about the prospective client, the better. The simple fact of knowing, for example, that your prospect must attend a lunch meeting the day of your presentation will keep you from requesting an appointment for 11 am. This way, the potential client won't have the excuse of 'having to go' and won't be able to say, 'I must cut you short'.

Get into the habit of doing your own market research. Take the time to examine why and how your product can be of use to your next prospect. Many sales have been lost in the past only because the salesperson did not have good product knowledge. For example, would you buy a word processor from someone who could not show you how to retrieve data from memory or who could not even type?

The better you know your product and your industry, the more creatively you will sell. Keep your mind open to new marketing concepts. Then you will leave the ranks of the average salesperson. Clients will listen to your recommendations and will show respect for your know-how. Your sales volume will increase as soon as people begin telling each other about your knowledge of the facts and figures.

Summary

1. Read everything you can about selling: the psychology of selling, selling techniques, the methods of successful salespeople. Set aside a fixed hour every day for studying.
2. Know all the 'ins and outs' of the service or product you are selling.
3. Do your own market research.
4. Keep your mind open to creative marketing ideas and suggestions and tips on selling.
5. Perfect your selling techniques, using the most modern tools available. Learn from your own mistakes and the mistakes of others.
6. Practise what you have learned and keep on learning.

Chapter 4

The First Steps

The knowledge you have acquired through:

- your education
- your exchanges with colleagues
- your own observations
- your practical experience

will help you to develop your ability right from the start.

The only way you can make faster progress than your competitors is to develop the following good habits early in your selling career. After acquiring know-how, you must:

- develop a positive mental attitude
- increase your self-confidence
- elaborate a working agenda and follow it
- work hard, but pace yourself.

Let's look at these one by one.

A positive mental attitude

A positive mental attitude and good working habits go hand in hand. Many of our attitudes and habits are acquired early in life. If negative attitudes and bad working habits have been part of your life up to this point, it is necessary to develop optimism about future success and to think positively. Then you will be motivated to change bad working habits to good ones. I used five basic steps to improve my own habits, early in my selling days:

1. I actively looked for all the responsibilities I could handle.
2. I often took the initiative. I didn't wait for anyone to come and tell me what to do next. I went ahead to the best of my ability and tried to improve my record.
3. I took chances. I always looked for opportunities.
4. I learned to make quick decisions. I often noticed that many who hesitated got nowhere. Right or wrong, I forced myself to make a decision on the spot.
5. I always tried to improve my knowledge and education outside my own speciality. I questioned, read, learned, watched and questioned again.

A person becomes what he or she wants to become. All human beings are self-made. But only the successful ones will admit it. The key to success can never be found in books, courses or seminars. It lies in your attitude. As you grow older, you discover that it is your attitude alone that will determine your achievements.

Don't ever let anyone tell you that they can motivate you. To my knowledge this has never been successful. Only you can motivate yourself! Sales managers and trainers can show you how to become self-motivated, but they cannot go to work for you.

Let's stop and think for a moment. What could give you the will to succeed? How might you develop your personal capabilities? Some of us are successful and others not. Why? Are some of us intelligent and others not? Maybe some are gifted and others not. Does 'Lady Luck' have anything to do with it? Would a positive, healthy attitude be helpful? What about hard work, constant effort, study and self-discipline? In my opinion, a person's success is determined by a healthy, positive attitude and willingness to learn. Intelligence, giftedness and luck do not have much influence.

Are tests important?

I have tried a good number of psychological, IQ and graphological tests during my career, and all these provide a good measure of past performance. They define what you have learned and remembered. They may sometimes indicate a tendency, but certainly do not determine a natural disposition towards a given level of future performance.

Should the results of some of your tests not be satisfactory, do not despair, do not be discouraged and do not lose faith. Remember that any test you take can never define your potential or your future performance. Take heart, and remember: 'Those who think they can, will'. The ball is in your court. Everything depends on the way you see things and the way you do things. Some have stated that talent creates opportunities in life. I claim that the will to succeed creates opportunities as well as talent.

The optimist and the pessimist

Some will say, 'The glass is half-empty'; others will say, 'The glass is half-full'. Those who talk about the half-empty glass show a negative attitude. The 'half-full glass' believers are much more positive.

Let me give you another interesting definition of the optimist and the pessimist. Someone passed it on to me and I have used it ever since. 'An *optimist* is a person who sees an opportunity in every calamity; a *pessimist* sees a calamity in every opportunity.' Which of these two is more likely to succeed?

To motivate yourself and have a fulfilling career, you must:

1. Step away from fear, to self-confidence, courage and audacity.
2. Stop being a follower and start being a leader.
3. Move away from 'empty' words towards known facts and conviction.
4. Shake off the daily routine and take on the responsibilities and the challenge of a career.
5. Leap from lack of confidence to final accomplishment.

In the words of Gary Gariepy, one of the best confidence builders of this century, 'Forget the errors of your past; think only of your future and its potential'.

Wake up . . . and smile!

How can you change a negative attitude to a positive one? There's one easy way. Learn to smile and keep on smiling all day long! Practise hard, look at yourself in the mirror often. Learn to do it naturally.

I am sure that you remember a happy period in your life when you woke up eager to get to work. You left your home with a smile, because your heart felt like smiling and your spirit glowed in that early morning smile. If, for some reason, you no longer smile when you leave for work, you must do so again. You will climb the ladder of success more easily. Get up cheerfully and go at it with confidence. Never look back! Self-confidence and your smile will help you through the week.

As a child, do you recall how happy you felt getting up on Christmas Day? The night before, you had trouble falling asleep, hoping for and dreaming about the gifts you expected to get the next morning. A joyous feeling warmed your heart and cheer was all around. The next morning you woke up with a wide, happy smile. Nothing could keep you from jumping out of bed and peeking through the living-room doorway to find out what was under the tree.

Wouldn't it be marvellous to wake up with that same happy feeling 365 days a year? You, as a salesperson, have that opportunity. Every day can be Christmas again in your home! All 86,400 seconds of every day can be happy ones for you, because you are rendering a service and filling a need. Change your attitude now! Rise with a smile every morning, as if it were Christmas again and again. . .

To illustrate my point, let me remind you of an old story that you must have heard many times already. Three stone-masons were busy on a large building site. When asked what they were doing, the first one replied grouchily, 'I'm just carving these huge stones'. The second one said without a smile, 'I'm putting up this big wall'. The third, however, joyously responded, 'I am building a cathedral'.

Only one of these men is truly happy, the one whose optimism, *joie de vivre* and smile make you understand that he is participating in the creation of a masterpiece. You, too, will notice a big change in your life as soon as you start smiling daily!

Let me suggest this simple test to prove my point. The very next time your phone rings, start smiling before you pick up the receiver, and keep on smiling as you say hello. The caller will feel your smile as it is transmitted through your voice and will be favourably impressed. Next time *you* call someone, try it again! As you practise, you will soon notice an improvement.

All your telephone conversations will become pleasant. Appointment-making will be easier, since your prospects will feel more inclined to give you a hearing and your clients will be happier.

Keep smiling, your future is in your hands!

Increase your self-confidence

Success in life comes to those with self-confidence. I discovered early in my career that one of the easiest methods of acquiring self-confidence was to speak in public. I soon noticed that many salespeople fail in our business because they don't know how to express themselves or state their ideas clearly. Even if you have all the knowledge you need, it won't help you if you cannot express yourself. Good speech habits are a must for all, including beginners.

Many clubs, associations and organisations ask their members to speak at lunches and dinners. I strongly suggest that you join one of these if you are not yet a member. In some cases, professional help is required. Many courses in public speaking and improving self-confidence are available.

As an instructor, I noticed that the trainees who lacked self-confidence were most often those who (1) were physically handicapped, (2) lacked technical knowledge or (3) had poor working habits. With practice, however, anyone with these disadvantages can become more confident. A second group required even more coaching: those who were (1) lazy, (2) unsure of themselves or (3) poor dressers.

Self-confidence is the key to achievement.

Draw up an agenda and follow it

If you want to increase your sales, keep a written list of things to be done. All professionals and successful salespeople keep an agenda. Start yours as early as possible in your career. Your days must be planned. Keeping an agenda will make things easier for you.

When you leave home in the morning, you should know

exactly where you are going. Your selling efficiency will increase greatly if you stick to your plan. If the product or service you offer is best sold in the home, you should make evening appointments. If you are selling to a married couple, make sure that both husband and wife will be there. The evening appointment should be requested either the day before or that same morning. Work at your schedule. Enormous advantages can result if you are able to plan your weeks, months or even seasons ahead of time.

The Boy Scouts' motto, 'Be Prepared', applies to the sales profession too. Keep daily notes: write them down or dictate them into a cassette in your car immediately after you leave a client's office or home. Having this information at your fingertips will increase future sales. Professionals now use personal computers to store data about their clients, prospects and families. PCs are now a *must* in our profession.

Check the contents of your briefcase often, and always check it in the morning before you leave home. This way you will always be sure that you have all the paperwork and supplies you need for the day ahead. It's also important to remember to replace any items, samples, etc, you have left with your last prospect. I have often been embarrassed to find I was missing an item that I wanted to leave with a client.

If you use displays, samples or demonstration units to sell your product or service, always make sure they are in good working order. Preventive maintenance on your car can also keep you from losing time and therefore money.

If you need to travel through areas where there is heavy traffic, take this into account when setting up your timetable. Plan your meetings so that you spend as little time as possible on the road. Try to group calls for the same time period in one district. If you are in a large city, set up your morning and afternoon calls according to area. This will help you to avoid wasting time and perhaps having to cancel appointments.

Work . . . but pace yourself

About 25 years ago, Gary Gariepy told me, 'Remember, you must always work on your plan, but also plan your work'. To many, the word *work* is synonymous with tiredness, fatigue, weariness, exhaustion, dislike and even disgust! To you, it should mean *evolution, development, progress, outcome, pleasure, results, wealth* and *success*.

One of the best salespeople I have had the pleasure of knowing once told me, 'This world is full of people who are ready; some are ready to work, and others are ready to let go'. When you learn to like your work, your workload will become lighter, and your task will become easier and more interesting.

In the opinion of most of the professional salespeople I have worked with, success is tied directly to the number of presentations given every week. Achievement comes to the persistent salesperson, the one who gives a set number of presentations every day. This number necessarily varies, and depends on the product or service being sold.

It is wise to spend your time and energy sensibly. Pace yourself. Don't plan too many appointments in one day. Work eight hours, rest eight hours and relax eight hours. While relaxing, you can read, plan, study, update records, play.

Summary

1. Only a positive mental attitude can give you the will to succeed.
2. You are the only one who can motivate yourself.

3. Wake up and smile!
4. Develop self-confidence. Believe in yourself! Go to work with confidence, spirit and a smile!
5. Plan your day, your week, your month, your season.
6. Work hard, but pace yourself.

Chapter 5

Be Well Organised

You have often heard the saying, 'A place for everything and everything in its place'. Even the most unmethodical or muddle-headed person can succeed in business by following this rule.

At a San Francisco Mutual Fund and Insurance Convention, I had the pleasure of meeting some of the best salesmen and saleswomen in North America. I was amazed to discover that the salesman of the year was working from a small office on the outskirts of his town. He had only one secretary and seldom required any extra help. His earnings were tremendous, however. When he was asked what methods he used to achieve success, he said that no one needed a large staff and office to earn good money in sales. The key to a large commission was 'to spend as little time as possible in the office and keep everything well organised'.

Your office must become your 'lab'. When in it, you should be preparing your 'formula' for the next day's sales. In my selling days I used to keep a small sign above my desk. It said, 'HOW MUCH MONEY AM I MAKING FROM MY PRESENT TASK?' The other item on my notice-board was a huge hand-drawn thermometer, which I will describe later. The money notice had its advantages. It made me spend as little time as possible in my office, and whenever I was in the office, if I started to daydream, it would bring me back to reality.

Useful documents and files

These suggestions for documentation and filing systems are based on an office without a computer. However, most of them can be adapted to personal computer files.

1. *A qualified prospect card.* On this card, you keep a record of various visits, objections and possibilities. If you do not like to work with card files, you can use bound notebooks. Those who object to cards feel they can be lost too easily. On the other hand, they can be discarded if necessary, where notebook entries have to be corrected.
2. *A client card.* All necessary information for new orders or renewals can be recorded on this card. Many professionals like to keep additional and sometimes personal data on these cards, so that they can send birthday greetings, congratulations, reminders, etc. First names of children and spouses are always helpful. It is also important to record hobbies and special interests. When a 'qualified prospect' becomes a client, his or her card is moved to the client file.
3. *A correspondence file* for each new client should be opened as soon as after-sales servicing begins.
4. For some products and services, *old qualified prospect* cards can be useful. In low seasons or difficult times, names can be reviewed. If circumstances have changed, your product may have become more affordable or more interesting to some prospective clients who were not previously interested.
5. *A list of leads* is essential. The names on this list are transcribed on to 'qualified prospect' cards as soon as the person has been visited.

6. *A follow-up file* is helpful. Some prospects will ask you to come back at a later date. You will have asked, of course, 'Would you prefer September the 1st or shall we make it the 15th?' The date should then be recorded in the follow-up file.
7. Simplified *accounting ledgers*. In these you will enter sales, commissions, advances, expenses and all other financial records.

Personal statistics

Personal statistics are most useful in different selling situations. I have always found it very helpful to spend two or three hours at the end of each month reviewing my own sales records and getting the most out of them. You will find that some of these statistics may be useful to you too.

1. Determine from your statistics your most efficient *selling time* of the day. I discovered that I had much better closing skills in the early morning than in the late afternoon. Maybe my prospects were a tired bunch or perhaps I had more energy and conviction in the morning.
2. Find out the *job classification* of your clients. My experience showed that I had more success closing engineers and technicians, probably because of my background and because we 'spoke the same language'.
3. Discover the best *season* of the year for your kind of sales. By applying more effort at certain times, you can easily compensate for slower periods. In a cold country, people buy more cars in the spring. A good car salesperson will therefore take holidays in the winter.
4. Determine the best *advertising media* for your product. Did your ads bring more leads than your telephone appointments or were your direct mail flyers better still?

Summary

1. A place for everything and everything in its place.
2. Keep a neat filing system to store information on qualified prospects, clients and leads, as well as your own business finances.
3. Analyse your selling statistics monthly. Increased sales volume will result.

Chapter 6

Choose an Achievable Goal and Take Aim!

To outshine others and do wonders, people must pick a target or goal. The athlete's aim is to win the competition, just as the army general sets his sight on winning the battle and the war. When the salesperson starts his or her career, goal number one is usually large earnings. Other objectives can be equally important to different people. Let's name a few: public recognition, prestige, authority, political power, travel, cultural development. Any or all of these goals can motivate people to intensify their efforts and achieve success.

Most of our material and worldly goals depend on money. Wealth, or at least money, is necessary in today's society. Most salespeople therefore want to increase their sales in order to become wealthier. Even to reach other goals, money is often necessary. Attaining a prestigious social position, for instance, is difficult if you are penniless.

When I started selling, my manager suggested that I pick a realistic target. At the time, I felt like driving that year's nicest sports convertible and went to a nearby dealer to price it. I walked away with a tempting colour brochure, which I pinned to my wall immediately. Next to it I placed the huge hand-drawn thermometer that I mentioned in Chapter 5. I put the car price at the top of the thermometer.

After each sale, I would colour the mercury of my

thermometer, so that it represented half the commission I had earned that day. (The other half I set aside for regular expenses and savings.) I was amazed at the 'push' this gave me in my ambition to drive that magnificent car. Seeing the mercury rise week after week, it took only a few months before I was able to afford my dream car. I must be honest and tell you that I never purchased that beauty, because a convertible two-seater was far from practical in business. Also, by then, I had more ambitious objectives.

My target had ben reached and my goal achieved. That was the essential purpose of the realistic target. I was satisfied, I had progressed, my sales volume was up and I felt proud to have saved enough money to buy that nice car. Having reached my goal, I had even forgotten my lazy disposition. I had worked harder and more often, just because I kept looking at that beautiful brochure and the rising mercury on the wall.

This personal experience came in handy at a later date when I started showing beginners that a target had to be attainable in order to bring results. The balance between the possibility of reaching your goal and doing so too easily has to be weighed carefully. In other words, never pick a target that cannot be reached or one that can be reached too easily. Both are demotivating.

Let me pass on to you an important insight I received from my psychology instructor when I asked, 'Would you consider it a sign of weakness if someone gave up their dream or ambition?' He replied, 'For some, to give up may mean good judgement and could prove strong will'. I want you to realise that choosing an unattainable goal or reaching for the moon can easily result in total disillusionment or disenchantment. Frequently, vanity and stubbornness will force a person to go on. In fact, I have always found it far more difficult to get someone to give up if he or she was not making any headway in our profession than to recruit new trainees. This goes against the saying, 'Quitting is the hardest habit in the world to break.' In the sales profession, it is difficult to get someone who is unsuccessful to abandon the habit.

In order to set a financial goal, the professional will not dream of reaching for the moon, but will use good sense to set realistic goals. You must always set a tangible target, one that can be reached within reason. When working for commission only, you can solve the problem of the 'yearly income' by doing the following calculation:

1. Write down the actual number of sales you have made in the last 12 months.
2. Write down the number of actual presentations made during the same period. (Be truthful!)
3. Divide the number of sales into the number of presentations. This gives you your own *average sales per presentation.*
4. Divide your gross yearly income by the number of sales made to obtain your *average earning per sale.*

Statistics show that an average salesperson will close one sale out of every *five* presentations given. A trainee must usually make *ten* presentations to get one sale (not because the trainee knows anything yet, but because one out of ten people *want* to buy the product or service anyway). A well-trained professional can usually sell *one* out of every *three* prospects. These are facts.

Let us assume now that the product or service you sell pays you an average of £300 per sale. If it takes you *five* presentations to make *one* sale, each of the presentations you give is worth £60, *whether you make a sale or not!*

If you make only *three* presentations per working day, you will have earned £180, quite apart from the number of sales closed that day! If you work only 250 days per year, you will earn £180 × 250 = £45,000 per year.

Let's reverse the question. Say that you want to earn at least £60,000 gross commission per year. If in your industry the average earning per sale is £300, you must give at least 1000 presentations in 12 months (£60,000 = £60 × 1000). If you only want to work 250 days per year, this means *four* presentations per day at least.

To increase your earnings, you must simply improve your skill (not work any harder!). Instead of closing *one* sale for every *five* presentations, try for *one* out of every *three*. This means that every time you sit down with a prospective client, you will have earned £100, even if no sale results from the interview.

If you work 250 days per year, making *four* presentations per day, you will show gross earnings of 4 × £100 × 250 = £100,000.

All these are short-term goals. The long-term goal of your career should be satisfaction through professional improvement.

Summary

1. Set your own goals. Success will come more easily as you strive to reach a goal.
2. Pick a tangible target. Don't try to reach for the moon.
3. For the long term, try for a progressive increase in earnings.
4. Calculate your own revenues for each presentation given. Try to increase your sale-per-presentation ratio. In this way you'll be able to increase your earnings without having to wait for higher commissions from your employer.

Part 2

Put Your Best Foot Forward

Chapter 7

How to Overcome Stage Fright

All salespeople are afraid to face their first prospect. Performers, athletes, actors, singers and many others are also frightened before performing. As with the actor, the salesperson has stage fright. It is known that the very best salespeople continue to have this apprehension throughout their careers.

Before the big race at a track event, the distance runner will take several mental practice runs before warming up on the field. He will actually 'see' himself in the starting blocks and will run the race in his mind's eye, preparing himself and examining all possibilities. Rain or shine, he will be ready.

In the same way a salesperson must 'see' the whole sale before sitting down with the prospect. Just like the actor or singer, the salesperson goes over the part (even out loud) before the curtain goes up. This kind of preparation gets rid of stage fright.

My supervisor amazed me in my early days of selling. During my training period, when we reached his prospect's home or office he started whistling a well-known tune from the time he locked his car to the precise moment that he rang the client's bell. At first I paid no attention, but after three or four presentations before which he whistled the same tune, I caught on. This was his way of overcoming stage fright.

You can do it!

There is a little word called 'if' that is found in all languages. Although it is short, it can imply all sorts of conditions, suppositions or hypotheses. Conditions can, in turn, demonstrate doubt. And, as you know, doubt induces confusion and confusion will not lead to success. We must therefore eliminate all the 'ifs' from our lives. This will allow us to be mentally emancipated, to achieve success and avoid failure. Without 'ifs' and with willpower, you can reach your goal and get the things you want.

If we can learn to eliminate doubts and fears early, we are ahead! The most common negative thoughts that impede salespeople are:

- fear of failure
- fear of others.

A great number of salespeople I have worked with explain that they were afraid they would be thrown out of the home or office of their first prospects. This is the kind of fear that can affect your self-respect for a long time. After I started teaching my selling methods to others, I conducted a survey in various countries. I was pleasantly surprised to discover that no one has ever heard of any salesperson who had been physically ill-treated by a client. I hope this personal survey will help you to overcome all fears of altering the statistics on this subject!

Try to avoid thinking about your innate capabilities. These thoughts have unfortunately made some people permanently apprehensive about whether they can or cannot do certain things. Very few agree when I state that no one is born 'anyone' or 'anything'. However, it is true that no medical doctor has ever been born a doctor, nor has any solicitor been born a solicitor. Any normal newborn baby could grow up to become a good electrical engineer if his or her upbringing, family surroundings, early environment and willpower had encouraged that.

You can do it if you never think or imagine that you are limited in your capacity to learn, produce or better yourself in order to achieve success. If you keep thinking along these lines, you will eliminate your apprehension even if limited stage fright persists throughout your career.

Summary

1. Eliminate the 'ifs' in your daily thinking.
2. Think positively. Never be afraid of others or of failure.
3. Before your next appointment, make a mental videotape of your next sale.
4. Keep saying to yourself: I can do it! And do so! Remember: you are what you think you are!

Chapter 8

Be Pleasant and Friendly

How many times have you passed a shop window and noticed an item you liked? Once inside, you were suddenly confronted by an unfriendly salesperson. Without hesitation, you turned round and left the shop empty-handed. That salesperson just missed a sale!

It is helpful to remember that in the selling profession, when you come face to face with a prospective buyer, that buyer, too, could be 'put off' or unfavourably impressed. Remember that first impressions are usually lasting ones and that success or failure depend on you alone.

We all prefer to buy from 'nice', friendly people, rather than grouchy ones. It is a fact that many housewives change supermarkets, dry-cleaners and other service businesses if they don't find happy, pleasant employees working there.

We must learn how to make a favourable impression before explaining the product or service we sell. This first impression could be lightning-quick or it could take minutes to sink in. Whatever the time period, the impact must be positive and the best possible. There is no getting away from it!

From the beginning, think only about your prospect's needs. Your own benefit, profit and welfare come second to those of the potential client. As clients ourselves, we always feel closer to people who are interested in our well-being and who are willing to look after us if necessary. All professionals act this way, and their actions and speeches are never cunning or calculated.

A good salesperson tends naturally to like others and is looking forward to trying to please people. You will have a spectacular career if you can show your prospects and clients that you truly like them and appreciate them. Although it is sometimes difficult to remain unselfish and to put your clients' interests first, you will be much better off if you can adjust to this way of thinking early in your career.

When I started selling, one of my first clients kept insisting that he wanted to take up two investment schemes that day: one in his wife's name and one for himself. I complied with his request, but that night, while entering my client's data, I noticed with surprise that the sales charges on two separate schemes were much higher than on a single larger one. Early the next morning, I returned to my client's office and showed him how I could save him more than 20 per cent in charges by converting his two schemes into one single one. He thanked me and accepted my suggestion. Evidently, he never knew that my commission was seriously reduced. Over the years he remained grateful, and my early loss was well compensated by the number of friends he referred to me.

Many, if not all, salespeople know that clients' needs come first, but we all have a tendency to forget this. In order to be pleasant, obliging and kind at all times, *do to others what you would like others to do to you.*

Do not find fault

None of us likes to be criticised. Therefore, do not find fault with others and try not to correct your prospects. A clothing salesman I once interviewed said, 'I would never criticise the suit a man was wearing when he entered my shop, even though I thought it looked awful. Surely he must have liked it when he had it made. It would be humiliating for him if I criticised it now, and he would probably leave. Instead, I usually guide him through my shop's selection without mentioning the suit'.

This principle can be applied to all types of selling. As an example, if you sell insurance, you would never approach a prospect and tell him that the policy he held was of little value. This would be as bad as saying, 'Sir, what a stupid decision you made 12 years ago! You should have been smarter!' Even if you did not really say that, the result would be the same. By criticising his present policy, you would be touching a sensitive nerve. He would become touchy and irritable, and you would lose a sale.

Never argue

Whenever possible, avoid discussions, debates and arguments. Keep all discussions and expressions of opinion for your private life. Of course, you will have your own thoughts on a particular subject, but always *let the prospective client tell you how he feels*. Your mind must be geared to one thought only: I am here to *sell to this prospect*. If you start arguing, you will not convince the prospect to buy, nor will you be able to close the sale. Always respect your client's ideas on every subject. You do not necessarily need to have the same opinion, but what does that matter – if you make the sale!

To 'live in harmony with others' must be a prime objective of all salespeople. If you are irritable and often become angry or incensed, you should work alone, where you don't need to come in contact with other people. Jobs fitting this description are difficult to find!

Salespeople offer their wares and services to a variety of human beings. Some are nice and gentle; others aggressive and far from polite. Whatever the reception, the professional must remain cool, polite and patient if results are to be obtained. If you smile and react pleasantly, communication will be established and defences will be pulled down. Ill-humoured, moody people usually come around when they see a smiling face. Just like a yawn, a smile is contagious.

If prospective clients do not 'take to you', chances are slim that they will buy your product, and they won't make an effort to become likeable either. Reaching your goal in this case is most difficult. You have a slight chance of turning the situation around if you find something about your prospect that you can honestly admire. Truthful admiration and esteem are conducive to getting on with people. This, in turn, can lead to a warming up of the interview or presentation. If this warming can finally lead to the ice being broken, your chances of closing the sale will improve a lot.

Good humour and kindness will disarm hostility and will lead you to more and bigger sales.

Summary

1. We all prefer to buy from 'nice' people and people who smile.
2. Show sincere interest in prospective clients.
3. Remember that the client's needs come first. Yours come last.
4. Do to others what you'd like others to do to you.
5. Do not criticise.
6. Never argue. The client is always right.
7. Stay cool and pleasant! Keep in mind: 'I am here to close a sale!'

Chapter 9

Well Dressed but Different!

During one of the recruiting drives at our head office, the receptionist rushed into my office to say that someone very special had arrived for his appointment. She looked so taken aback that I asked her to show the applicant in immediately. The man who entered was well dressed, wearing a dark suit and a silk turban with a matching tie. He was smiling openly and his neatly trimmed beard couldn't hide his jovial personality. Originally from New Delhi, this young engineer quickly became one of our top producers. Not many could resist the temptation to talk to him, and most prospects listened to him closely.

This experience convinced me more than ever that 'being different', besides being well dressed, was essential in order to be more successful than others. When a salesperson approaches you, what does a cursory glance tell you? First you notice the clothes, and that first impression will be there for good. Your memory probably registers details such as shoes, tie, hair, face, smile, hands and more. Your mind has now been stamped, imprinted with this impression.

Whatever the effect of that first impression – good, bad or indifferent – it will stay there, and your subconscious will always associate that first glimpse with that person. Please remember that this also applies to you when you first meet a prospect. Never underestimate the value of being well dressed, and try to add that extra touch to be slightly different. Never exaggerate, however.

We all tend to remember the person with that slight 'difference'. The difference could even be an unusual name or nickname. Think back for a few seconds: do you remember the salesman who sold you a car five years ago? What was special about the person who sold you your life insurance policy ten years ago? How about the saleswoman who came to the door selling encyclopedias? Surely you remember a certain salesperson. Why him or her? Was it because of the small difference?

Even a person who does not remember your name might say, 'Oh, yes, the one who always wore boots', or again, 'Yes, I remember the gentleman who smoked those small cigars.' The client might even say, 'He always wore a nice tiepin' or 'She always had beautiful silk scarves'.

Follow the latest fashion when you dress, but do it with restraint. Never overdo it. The money you spend on your wardrobe will be well worth your while, and many sales will result from it. Become the *distinguished salesperson*, but never the odd one.

Your voice is important!

Many salespeople get into the habit of giving boring presentations. They know their product well, but they become bored telling people about it every day. Their delivery becomes dull, and many prospects simply stop listening. Some I have heard even remind me of a vicar I knew who used to put his flock to sleep, never varying the pitch or volume of his voice or the tone of his speech.

Our profession is not always easy, because when we become tired we can easily slip into dullness – and then our sales start slipping too. How can we overcome this difficulty? By always listening to our own voices and presentations and being attentive to the reactions of our clients and prospects.

All professionals use tape recorders to improve their speech. With these wonderful machines, you can learn to speak with more conviction and change pitch and intonation. Never become monotonous! Try to react: speak with briskness and vivacity, but *never speak too fast*! Your prospect has to clearly understand everything you are saying. Keep in mind that *you* know your product well, but that the prospect has maybe never even heard of it until you came along. Prospects have to know what they are buying if you want them to become clients.

Try to be articulate at all times. Do not garble words and phrases. Pronounce all your words distinctly. Use simple words and make sure they are clear and precise.

Some colloquial words and expressions may help you in your sales, but if you picked them up from someone else, make sure you adapt them to your own personality. Never try to put one over on someone. That's unprofessional and it won't sell much. Clients won't usually be fooled by 'fast talkers'.

The other side of the coin is bad too. Avoid becoming a teacher or instructor. Do not flood your prospect with technical data, for instance. You do not want him or her to become a technician. You want a client. As such, the prospect might never need to know the technical details. In fact, some of them might be a turn off. In most cases, a prospect is not going to buy unless you can show that it is in his or her interest to do so. Knowing everything you know about the product may not convince the prospect to buy it at all!

If you are able to *speak well by saying as little as possible* you will be a tremendous salesperson. Be *clear* and *precise*. You will sell *better* and *more*.

Summary

1. It is important to be well dressed. Dress in the latest fashion, but with elegance and restraint.
2. Wear something distinctive, different – but don't overdo it. Don't be odd.
3. The first impression you make will be the lasting one.
4. Train your voice. Use a tape recorder and listen to yourself often.
5. Speak with conviction and vivacity, but never talk too fast.
6. Never give a lecture. Speak well, but talk little.

Chapter 10

O Empathy!

The word 'empathy' originates from the Greek *empatheia*, meaning affection, and *pathos*, or feeling. It is a key word in selling psychology. I have always used the following example to explain empathy to sales trainees.

During World War II, anti-aircraft gunners used heavy machine guns and anti-aircraft guns. Both of these fired shells and bullets. If the gunner did not make a proper calculation of the aircraft's speed and height or the speed of the wind, he could fire his cannon until he had used up all his ammunition without ever hitting the plane. This gunner could be compared to a salesperson *without empathy*: a person who doesn't understand 'how the prospect is feeling' at any given moment.

On the other hand, the salesperson *with empathy* can be compared to today's anti-aircraft gunners. They fire rockets of different types. Some of these are attracted to and follow the heat emission of the aircraft's jet engines. The plane can take all kinds of evasive actions: it can fly faster, turn, climb, dive or slow down, but the rocket follows it until it hits the plane. The rocket image is the one the professional salesperson should use in 'navigating' the prospect until the sale is made final. If the prospect is in a hurry, the salesperson cannot lose any time. If, on the other hand, the prospect is fully relaxed, the salesperson is calm and unhurried, not agitated or excited.

Empathy is certainly not an innate quality. It can only be 'acquired' by someone who is willing to learn it and practise it. Most of us need a lot of will power and desire to master it. In my opinion, those who use it with success have learned to do so from their colleagues. Empathy cannot be picked up from books or manuals!

Let me give you an example in which empathy helped me to close two sales. A woman phoned our office and requested that one of our salespeople call at her home that same evening. Our receptionist was unable to locate anyone who was free that evening, so she turned to me for advice. I decided to take the call myself and went to the address I had been given. It was a shoe-repair operation. Since it was after hours, I knocked on the door, and a man came to open it. Before I had a chance to introduce myself fully, a woman yelled from the back: 'Who is it, Arthur? . . . Make sure you lock the door!' At that moment, my instinct (or empathy) whispered: 'Make sure you give your presentation to the woman of the house, because you know who wears the trousers in this household!' I concluded the sale the same evening.

Interestingly enough, when I returned two weeks later for my service call, I closed a second sale by suggesting to the woman that it would be in her husband's interest to become a client as well. It didn't take long for her to 'suggest' this to her spouse. In fact, that day she practically made the sale for me.

Summary

1. Empathy is the faculty of adapting your personality to others to create better understanding.

2. You can develop better empathy with others, through effort and practice.
3. Without empathy, no one can be a huge success in sales.

Chapter 11

What's in a Handshake?

You might have smiled when you read the title of this chapter. You might even have asked yourself, 'What do I need to know about handshakes?' In Europe and South America, handshakes are important, and in France people shake hands with other people at least four times a day. This is true in Italy as well. In North America, however, handshakes are not as common as they are in Europe.

I discovered the art of handshaking when I went to Europe for the first time. I was amazed to see people shaking hands when they arrived at the office in the morning, when they left for lunch at noon and again when they came back from lunch and left work in the evening. At home in Canada, people shook hands only when they met someone for the first time or when they met a friend they hadn't seen for some time. I was so astonished at first that I started to make notes on the people I met, trying to guess their personalities from their first handshake. What had started as a game soon became a study. The following are some of the observations I have made on how different handshakes reflect personality. You can be the judge of how useful they are to you.

The flabby hand. When a person offers you a limp, soft paw, you have the distinct impression of shaking hands with overcooked pasta! The owner of such a weak hand usually has a negative outlook on life and does not look forward to the future with interest. I have noted a number of pessimists who shook hands this way. Younger men and women who hid their eyes behind dark or reflective glasses also tended to shake hands like this.

The hesitant handshake. This greeting belongs to people who seem to be unsure whether or not they should actually offer you their hand. Sometimes they wait for you to stretch out your hand first. Only then will they offer theirs. In other words, they wait for you to make the first move. These people are often undecided about their direction in life or in business.

The squeezing handshake. The person who squeezes your hand like a bench vice seems to enjoy hurting you. He (it's usually a man) appears to be wicked and to want to show you his strength. Maybe he simply wants to show off his muscles and his body. He might be emotionally insecure, and you shouldn't be surprised if he is trying to overcome an inferiority complex. Some even cultivate their muscles to make up for everything they think they are missing in life.

The 'next-to-the-body' handshake. I discovered this type of handshake by watching the news on television. It is usually used by politicians or powerful party leaders. One of the greatest and tallest of the French presidents resorted to it all the time. The arm and elbow are bent, and the hand stays near the trousers pocket on the right-hand side. People who use it are on the lookout. They watch their own moves and are careful. They appear to be conservative and unwilling to take risks.

The impelling handshake. This one is impulsive and is used by people who never miss an opportunity to shake your hand. As soon as they meet you, they thrust their hand forward and shake yours with vigour. Experts view these people as insecure and afraid of not being accepted by other members of society.

The non-gripping handshake. This one is different from the flabby handshake described above, in that it is really no handshake at all. The hand is thrust forward, but it's rigid. The fingers don't move much – they don't really seize your hand. I have noticed that most users of this handshake seem to be communicating the message: 'I don't want to get involved with you'. This handshake tends to be used more by women than by men.

The robot's handshake. The robot offers his hand automatically and very swiftly. Often, he won't even notice that he has shaken your hand. He is totally unconcerned and indifferent. People who use this handshake are first and foremost interested in themselves and in looking after their own objectives. They go by without seeing other people and will sometimes fail to notice a person after shaking hands with him or her.

The jackhammer. This one feels like a pneumatic drill: your hand is pumped up and down, with the handshaker's hand acting like a piston, firmly raising and lowering yours. Most people who use this handshake have a lot of willpower, but may also be inflexible in their lifestyle.

The 'prison' handshake. The 'prison' handshaker holds your hand without giving it back to you. You can hardly shake it loose. You can only get it back when he is certain he has captured your full attention. Be careful! This type of handshake may be that of an opportunist or someone who would like to manipulate you into making a certain decision.

The normal handshake. This one differs from all those I've just described. Open, frank, candid, honest, it will initiate good relations, good kinship and perhaps love. You will never fail to notice it, nor will you misinterpret it when it is offered to you.

Although it may seem unbelievable, you can help your career along if you can recognise the message being given through a handshake. You should always adapt your approach, depending on the person's handshake. Who knows, in some cases this method could help you close a sale faster.

- If you face an *opportunist*, you could talk about the circumstances of your encounter and eventually the good fortune of your being there, selling your product.
- Facing a very *determined prospect*, it is useful to be more determined than he or she is.
- If you can show that your product is indispensable to a person who is *interested only in himself or herself*, you will increase your chances of making a sale.
- Making the decision to buy on behalf of the *indecisive type* might be useful (but very difficult!).
- You can help someone who feels *insecure* by offering him or her your product. Lack of self-confidence does not mean that the prospect will not buy from you, but you may have to insist more than usual.
- If possible, reassure the *pessimist* before doing anything else. Your sale will come more easily.
- Sometimes you will have to *flatter* a prospect who likes to be flattered. He or she will be happy, and you will be glad to have made the sale.

Responding to different 'handshake messages' will help you to increase your empathy with the potential client.

Summary

1. Learn to recognise the messages being given by different types of handshake.
2. Use 'empathy' to improve your selling skills, by adapting your approach to the messages given by each different prospect.
3. The observation and study of human behaviour will help you in your professional career.

Chapter 12

Face to Face . . .

The first words you say to your prospect are often the key to success or failure. What you say and how you say it will be affected by how you feel just before you meet the potential client. If you are tense or annoyed, your prospect will naturally not be as interested in speaking to you. Unfortunately, one of the things that often makes us tense and annoyed is waiting, and salespeople have to do a lot of waiting. Most of the waiting is done outside the prospect's office. It's easy to become impatient if the wait is long. We all have a tendency to get tense, and if a client is delaying, we might start asking ourselves, 'Who does he think he is, anyway?' or 'She can't get away with treating me like this!'

If you happen to be nervous, you will go through different stages of feeling. At first you may feel dejected, later you may become impatient, and then you will be annoyed. When your prospect's door opens at long last, you may have reached the hostile stage. At this point you will probably try to calm yourself down by thinking, 'I am furious, but I won't let it show'. Think again! Feelings of this nature cannot be hidden. In spite of all your efforts, your aggressiveness will show and your prospect will feel it. Of course, this will start things on the wrong foot and you'll end up with no sale.

I would like to suggest another approach. Prepare yourself

the way all good athletes do. While you are waiting, start warming up. Use the waiting area to stage your presentation mentally. Start running that videotape in your mind. Decide what strategy you are going to use.

I have often noticed that a new prospect's personality can be discerned at least in part from the pamphlets and notices or even diplomas displayed in the waiting room next to his or her office. Do a guessing game while you're waiting. Then, once you are let in for the interview, see how accurate your guesses were.

If you are able to wait patiently and calmly, it will send the message that the service or product you are selling is worthwhile. It will show that you are confident in it and in yourself.

Your time is money

Sometimes when you arrive for an appointment you will find that your prospect has been called away on an emergency. The managing director has called her into a meeting at short notice or she is fighting a deadline to submit a bid. In cases like these, your wait might be quite long. Since your time is money, you cannot wait for ever, but can you leave the office without jeopardising your sale?

I have often said to receptionists or secretaries something along these lines: 'I am sorry, but I have another appointment in 20 minutes. Would you be sure to explain my predicament to your boss? I know he will understand. Could you give me another appointment for Thursday at 10 am?' If you let people know that your time is precious, they will respect you for it. In most cases, when I had to rearrange an appointment because my prospect was late or couldn't make it the first time, I usually had a slight advantage. He owed me one because he'd made me waste an hour on my last visit!

Choose the location with care

The setting of your presentation can make a big difference. Different settings will be better for different types of products and services. You will have to decide whether it is more appropriate to make your presentation in the prospect's home or in his private office, for instance. In my early days, I wouldn't hesitate to sit with a prospect in a huge, open office with dozens of people working nearby. But I soon changed my tactics when I saw I was not getting results. Once I was even taken to task by the personnel manager when my prospect's colleagues complained that I was disturbing them. From then on, I always asked for an appointment at home, *that same day*. 'Would 7 pm be convenient, or would you prefer 8 pm?' (Always give a choice; never, *but never*, ask: 'Would tonight be convenient?' This leaves the door open for a negative response.)

One place that is inappropriate for making a presentation is at a lunch meeting or dinner. Although I have always had difficulty convincing salespeople in France and other European countries of this, business lunches and dinners are fine for warming up prospects or getting them in the buying mood, but they are not good places to make a sale. I do not believe in taking out the order pad at coffee time. Prospects do not like to sign cheques on a cluttered restaurant table. Personally, I also find it difficult to talk with enthusiasm about my products when my mouth is full. Again, it is up to you to decide where you feel the most comfortable. For me, the choice has always been an office (the prospect's or mine) or the potential client's home or car.

I should add that I have often invited my better clients for a gourmet meal as a 'thank you' gesture. One even mentioned to a mutual acquaintance that it was a pleasure to do business with someone who had a bit of class, and not a person who baited his clients like fish.

Where to sit

If you are selling an intangible, you will often have to show your prospect notes. Should this be the case, may I suggest that you do *not* sit opposite him or her during the presentation. Sit beside your prospect. If you are right-handed, sit on the right side. If you are left-handed, sit on the left. This way, when you are writing and the potential client is trying to follow your notes, your writing hand will not hide your pad.

Many trainees do not know how (or are too shy!) to sit *next to* their prospect. In all probability, no one has shown them how to do it. Many may not think that this is even important. I believe it is *essential.* This apparently silly, insignificant factor might make all the difference in your selling career.

This is how I do it. In most offices, two chairs face the person's desk. You are supposed to sit in one of these. After you have broken the ice, you simply get up and *move your chair to the other side of the desk* and say gently, 'I am sure you won't mind me sitting next to you, as I have some interesting figures to show you. . .' By moving your chair while saying that you are doing so, you will already be sitting down before your prospect has a chance to respond. Don't worry – your prospect is not going to tell you to get back on the other side of the desk now that you are sitting beside her. But if you had asked beforehand, you would probably have got the answer, 'It's all right, stay where you are'. In that case, you would have had no choice but to stay put.

By sitting where you have decided you are going to sit, you are also showing your prospect that you are taking charge of the situation. *You* are the salesperson, *you* are in charge of explaining your product and *you* must take things in hand. If you cannot do so, you have lost the sale.

I once had the honour of being received by the financial assistant to the president of France in the Elysée Palace in Paris. I was accompanying the president of the French bank to which my corporation was giving technical assistance. We wanted to obtain permission from the French government to launch a direct sales force in France to initiate the sale of mutual funds (called SICAVs in France). It was a most important meeting – a do-or-die kind of thing for the bank's proposal.

The office was huge, and the visitors' chairs were about ten feet in front of the assistant's desk. I horrified my friend the bank president when, in the middle of the meeting, I got up and started moving my heavy chair next to this gentleman. After we left, he was flabbergasted that the assistant had not reprimanded me or asked me to return to my original position in the middle of his office. Because of my method, the meeting was successful, our plan was approved, and mutual funds have been selling briskly in France ever since that memorable day.

During your next presentation, *try* my method. You will soon discover the advantages of sitting *next to* your prospect, rather than in front of the desk.

One last tip: if you are giving your presentation to two people at the same time, please make sure *never to sit between them*. By sitting to one side of *both* of them, you address yourself to both and will not have to move your head backwards and forwards between them.

Never try to sell in the living room: it is not a practical place to give a presentation. Remember, you need a table for the purchase order and cheque to be signed, and you can't do that on your knees in the living room! Getting the cheque signed is your purpose for being there. Don't forget it, and don't hesitate to 'tell' your clients so by taking the situation in hand right from the beginning.

You can say, 'Do you mind, Mrs Brown, if we sit at your dining-room (or kitchen) table? I have some important papers to show you'. In all my selling years, no one has ever refused. Where you sit is important – even if you don't think so now!

Summary

1. Learn to wait patiently, using that waiting time to prepare for the interview.
2. If you really cannot wait, leave! But make a new appointment before you go.
3. Always choose the best setting for your presentation.
4. Don't try to sell during a lunch or dinner. Close the sale before or after a meal.
5. Take the situation in hand by sitting next to your prospect, not on the other side of the desk or table.
6. Sit to the right of your prospect if you are right-handed (and to the left if you are left-handed).
7. When making a presentation to two people, never sit between them.

Chapter 13

Breaking the Ice

During any interview, the salesperson will reach the point where the ice must be broken and the presentation launched. The small talk ends and the serious selling begins. Many trainees are unable to get their prospect's complete attention right from the start and therefore lose their opportunity to leave the interview with a signed order form. Some have the bad habit of jumping into the selling part of the interview too quickly. (I have also had to teach myself not to do this.) Others never seem to get past the small talk and into the sale.

The selling experts have different opinions as to when the actual presentation should begin. Although you will never want to begin the presentation immediately, you must get the full attention of the prospective client right from the start. Then it will be easier to break the ice. Here are four ice-breaking methods that can be adapted to the particular service or product you are selling.

1. **Fear.** Many good salespeople use fear to get into the presentation.

- 'Sir, don't miss this opportunity. You might be sorry later if you do.'
- 'This flat will be sure to bring you a nice capital gain in a few years. Don't let it go. . .'

- 'House prices are expected to increase soon. You'll want to get into the property market now before they get any higher.'
- 'I'm sure you saw these terribly sad pictures of your competitor's fire loss the other day in the paper.'
- 'This is my very last one. I'm not sure I can get any more.'
- 'It's very dangerous, you know, to store petrol in your garage. This electric mower is safe and will please your family and neighbours because of its low noise level.'
- 'If you take this correspondence course, you might well be promoted first. But if you can't make your mind up to start today, it may be too late tomorrow.'

2. **Curiosity**. If I came to see you and said, 'By buying this service, you will double your annual income', you might be mildly interested, but you wouldn't be intrigued. But if I said, 'What do you think I'm hiding behind my back?' your curiosity would more likely be aroused and you would be more likely to give me your full attention.

   Of course, you will never go into a prospect's office and ask this question! Find a good opening phrase that will awake your prospect's curiosity, using the product or service that you sell. Let me warn you, however: don't ever ask your prospect a question to which he can answer no. If you do, you are wasting your time; you might as well go to your next appointment!

3. **Pride.** Some professional salespeople appeal to the pride and self-respect of the prospect. This can be difficult at times, but here are a few examples:

- 'Given your position, Mrs Black, you need the best suit available. I think this one might be appropriate. Would you like to try it on?'

- 'I can see that you take pride in your children and you would want to ensure that they have the best education. This school offers. . .'
- 'By making this donation today, you are ensuring that your name will be remembered. . .'
- 'Just imagine, sir, how proud your wife will be when you buy this most prestigious of cars.'

4. **Profit.** We all like to get a bargain. Even the wealthy are happy to profit from discounts or rebates.

- 'This heating system will save you hundreds over a period of. . .'
- 'If you add this line to the merchandise you already have available, your profits will soar. . .'
- 'This policy will save you pounds, and your cover will start immediately.'
- 'This dictating equipment will take the load off your present staff, and you won't be forced to take on extra personnel.'

Once you have captured your prospect's attention with ice-breakers like these, do not let his or her mind wander from the discussion. Start your presentation right away.

Be *brief, clear* and *precise*. Speak distinctly.

Summary

1. You must find the right moment to break the ice. Don't jump right into the presentation, but don't let the small talk run on too long.
2. To break the ice, you have to get the prospect's full attention.
3. The most effective ice-breakers appeal to the prospect's fears, curiosity, sense of pride, or desire to make a profit.

Part 3

Getting Down to Business

Chapter 14

Get the Prospect on Your Side

Some time ago, a good friend asked me, 'How would you sell a kitten to someone who never wanted a cat?' While thinking about the question, I answered that I had never yet had occasion to sell house pets, but . . . He cut me short and stated, 'Today I sold my cat's litter easily. I asked my son Peter to try selling the kittens to our close neighbours. I suggested leaving one in each house for the night. He was to return the next morning to take them back if no one wanted to buy them for £10. Instead, he came back with £60, since no one could stand the thought of parting with that tiny animal after having spent the night caring for it. The kitten had become part of the family. . .'

Without knowing it, my friend had used one of the most powerful sales tools available: *creative selling*. He had awakened his clients to their need of or desire for his product.

Most sales are lost during the first 30 seconds of the interview. Think back! Do you remember any salespeople who were *unable* to sell you a product lately? They probably never even started to get you interested. It has been proved that for each sale lost because of lack of technical knowledge, ten sales are lost because of the salesperson's inability to whet the prospect's appetite.

People who sell business machines know that to make a sale, they have to leave demonstration units in their customer's office for several days. Once they are used, many of these marvels become indispensable . . . and the sale is closed!

Not long ago, someone came to our house trying to sell me a season ticket for a private box at the local football ground. No one can deny that football is a fascinating sport, but I personally happen to prefer tennis. The salesman just wasted his time because he did not try to discover my preference. No one will hide their taste in sports; it is an easy subject to discuss. It helps to do your homework. Find out what your prospect's tastes are early in the interview – or before, if possible, by checking with people who have referred the prospect to you. As you develop the skill to discover your prospect's preferences, your salesmanship will rise above the average.

Awaken your prospect's need or desire

Early in my selling days, I asked myself, 'Is it fair play to look for my prospect's weakest point and use that knowledge to my advantage?' I soon realised that (1) if I didn't sell him or her my service, my competitor wouldn't hesitate to do so, and (2) if my service satisfied my prospect's need or desire, I would be rendering a service.

In general, it makes sense to stimulate prospects' desire to buy. You can do this by discovering

- what they do during their spare time
- why your product could be attractive to them
- how your product can be of service to them
- how your product could reduce their workload or make their life easier
- what thrills your potential client, what makes him or

her 'tick': family, children, home, car, boat, pet, tennis, golf, bridge, business, etc.

Keep notes on these things; they will come in handy one day.

Family

Let's take the example of a prospect who is devoted to family. All animals protect their newly born. Humans love their children. If you are selling a product or service geared to young ones, you can hardly fail. As a rule, you will find that everything benefiting the family (cars, televisions, encyclopedias, holiday homes, holidays, recreational vehicles, etc) can be sold easily when you tune in to the prospect's wavelength – his or her desire to have the best for the children.

Most wives love their husbands and most husbands love their wives. So if you are selling a product or service that will benefit the prospect's spouse, you will have an immediate advantage. There are exceptions, however.

Many years ago, my brother, who was starting his career at my side, asked me to help him sell an insurance scheme to the couple living next door. When he closed the sale, the woman of the house left the room to make coffee. My brother, who was happily filling out the application form, reached the designation 'Beneficiary', and asked the husband the standard question, 'I assume that Mrs White will be your beneficiary. Could you spell her first name for me, please?' To our great surprise, the husband simply answered: 'No! My beneficiary will be Miss Mason'. My brother rushed to fill in the name and had him sign the papers before his wife returned with the coffee.

Please beware! Never assume that a man will always protect his wife or vice versa. You can almost always be certain about children, but you cannot be sure about the spouse. Try to avoid blunders!

Discovering your prospect's 'business' wavelength

If you discover what matters to your potential client in his or her business dealings, you will do wonders. Remember that people spend 40 to 60 hours per week doing business. If they enjoy it or if it is even a major factor in their life, you will be able to sell if you discover ways to make your presentation fit the business side of their life. Talk to your prospects about their business. Let them tell you what matters to them in their work.

Also, large corporations usually buy from salespeople who remain in constant contact with their buyers. Salespeople thus have every opportunity to keep abreast of the buyer's business. But salespeople often do not take advantage of the 'business' factor in making their presentations.

I once accompanied a young trainee as he went to make a presentation to the general manager of a tent manufacturing company. Following our general training rule, I let the trainee do all the talking as he made the presentation and tried to close the sale. My young friend was unable to close, and as we were leaving, I picked up the ball, feeling that the sale would otherwise be lost. I said, 'I read not long ago that thousands of youngsters are discovering the joys of outdoor living and are in fact doing a lot of camping. Is that true?' The manager turned to me and enthusiastically explained how much his business had developed in the past two years. We listened with great interest for about 20 minutes. Once he'd finished his lengthy monologue, we had the right opening to return to the presentation and, having tuned in to his 'business wavelength', we closed the sale.

Discovering hobbies

Hobbies are in fashion. Leisure activities are on the upturn. Salespeople should take advantage of this! Stamp collecting, antique collecting, coin collecting, skiing, tennis, skydiving, parachuting, golf, hunting, fishing – they are all becoming more popular. Millions love music, the arts, theatre.

Question your prospect with fact. Let your potential client tell you what she enjoys and is looking forward to. As you gain experience in 'hooking on to' that wavelength, you will find that when she starts talking about her own interests, she will become more receptive. She tends to forget her problems. Stress disappears. Take advantage of it!

Give appealing descriptions of your product or service

I have often said to my trainees: If I sent you out to sell lemons you could start yelling, 'Buy my lemons' or 'Lemons for sale!' But once you passed the trainee stage, you would say, 'Look how nice my lemons are!' or 'These lemons are yellow ripe!' When you reached the professional stage, you would say, 'Please feel this beautiful lemon. When you take it home and slice it, you'll see the sunshine spurt out of it and you'll have a taste of healthy lemon juice that's full of vitamins'. Admit it, when you read this last sentence, you could almost taste the lemon! This is how you have to awaken your prospect's need or desire.

Discover key phrases that will sell your product, and use them often!

Summary

1. If appropriate, leave samples of your product with your prospects for a while. It will be difficult for them to return a product that has become useful to them.
2. Try to capture your prospect's attention and appeal to his or her feelings early in the interview.
3. Let your potential client speak. That's how you'll learn things that will help you.
4. Discover your prospect's habits, likes and dislikes early in the interview – or before, if possible.
5. Find out what makes your prospect 'tick' and use key words to appeal to his or her wants and desires.
6. The family, business interests and hobbies are often of major importance to a prospect. Appeal to those interests.
7. Act with tact. Try to avoid blunders!

Chapter 15

To See Is to Believe

The easiest sales to conclude (if easy sales actually do exist) are tangible ones. If you sell products that people can touch, feel or at least see, you have a great advantage over colleagues who are selling intangibles. Eyes open the avenue to the brain. Yet many salespeople fail to take advantage of this wonderful fact.

It is known that humans remember only 20 per cent of what they hear. However, their minds register 60 per cent of what they *see* when explanations are given at the same time. It is also a fact that 85 per cent of a person's knowledge and skill is fed to the memory through the eyes, but only 7 per cent comes through the ears. (The rest comes through the other senses.)

We salespeople have a tendency to forget that it has taken us days, if not weeks, to learn all about the product or service that we sell. It is therefore impossible to *teach* our prospects anything during the few minutes of our presentation. We must *demonstrate* the *advantages* of our product and we have to learn to do so visually.

If you are *told* about a lovely retreat in the woods, the message reaches your ears only. However, if I *showed* you a cabin set among trees on the shore of a lake, you would get a vivid image of the place and retain the impression for a longer time.

To sell ideas and services as well as products, learn to use your pen. The messages you write with an attractive pen will stay with your prospect.

One of the best salespeople I know is a Lebanese man. His territory is the Middle East, where he sells in various emirates. He writes with a lovely gold pen – he buys several in London every second month. At the end of his presentation when it's time for the prospect to sign the order form, he looks his princely prospect in the eye and hands him his gold pen, saying, 'Would you prefer to use your pen or *mine*?' 'Invariably, they take my pen', he tells me, 'because they were admiring it throughout the presentation'. My friend then makes the magnanimous gesture of offering his gold pen to the newly acquired client. He doesn't care about the cost of the gold pen. His 'golden' commissions make it worthwhile!

Your pen can have a hypnotic effect if you use it with care. I have met another salesman who successfully brought his prospect's attention back to his worksheet with his pen. *Try* this method! When one of your next prospects loses her concentration or starts looking elsewhere, start moving your pen in front of her eyes in a natural way and then *slowly lower it* to your worksheet. You will see her eyes following the pen back to your explanation. It seldom fails! And it's neat and professional.

We know that corporations are willing to spend large amounts of money to advertise on television shows with high ratings. That is because when you *see* a product advertised, you feel like buying it. Why are there so many trade shows and exhibitions in every major city in the world? They allow buyers to see, admire, touch, test and try out new and old products alike. Those of us who learn to demonstrate and explain our products at the same time will progress faster than others.

Even if your service or product cannot be presented

visually, learn to *show* and *demonstrate* its *advantages* in writing! This will make you a pro in no time.

When I was working as a junior engineer in Northern Canada I remember meeting a truck salesman who came to see us out in the wilderness equipped with a visual presentation. He had made a film of all his new models (video had not yet been invented). Obviously, he could not have taken his whole fleet that far north to show it to us, but by taking a film rather than just the manufacturer's pamphlets, he increased his chances of getting the order.

Whatever your product or service, try showing it by using pictures, videotapes, slides, etc. Your sales volume will increase fast. I have often seen salespeople – some lazy, some forgetful – make their presentation without the visual aids their firm had provided at great expense. Don't forget: *seeing is believing!*

Summary

1. A visual presentation increases your chances of closing the sale, as knowledge is gained and retained more by sight than by hearing.
2. Television advertisements, trade shows and exhibitions are popular and effective because they allow visual presentation.
3. Even if your product or service cannot be shown, demonstrate its advantages visually – in images or in writing. Do it!
4. Write down everything you say and use your pen to capture your prospect's attention.
5. Never trust your prospect's memory. If the potential client wants to think about your presentation, let her keep your notes!

Chapter 16

Learn to Listen

I have often asked myself, 'Why do so many salespeople forget to listen?' When I give courses or seminars, I always ask my audience this question. I get a number of different answers:

- 'I'm in a rush to close my sale.'
- 'I'm afraid I'll lose my prospect's attention if I stop talking.'
- 'We are too wrapped up in ourselves to think of our clients' thoughts and feelings.'
- 'No one has ever told me that listening was important.'

I must admit that we trainers are often at fault. We teach *what you should and shouldn't say*, but we often forget to tell trainees that it is more important to *listen*.

We all know that anyone who is starting in sales is frightened, and I think that it's fright that makes us talk too much. The trainee is afraid of not knowing enough, of forgetting to say something or of not being able to answer the prospect's questions properly. He or she might also be afraid of looking foolish or being thanked and curtly asked to leave. So to avoid all these things, the trainee just keeps talking and talking.

Experience brings us the wisdom to listen! The sooner you can master this easy technique, the better you will sell.

My nicest sale was made on a sunny day in July. I sold 11 endowment schemes to one woman who I convinced that she should start one for each of her ten children. The volume of these added up nicely, and the commission earned that day was equal to what I used to make in three months as an engineer. What I did not realise that morning was that I owed my sale to my ability to listen to this woman's story.

She had been widowed not long before, through a tragic accident. After I had listened with compassion, it was fairly easy for me to suggest a scheme for her children that would take care of their further education and their future, even if she was without a regular income for the rest of her life. It was only at my next meeting in the office that I understood why I had successfully closed. My supervisor used my example to explain to the other sales staff the advantages of learning to *listen*. No one had told me that before!

Today I know that even the great mathematician Albert Einstein knew the advantages of listening. He once told a reporter the secret of his success, saying, 'SUCCESS = X + Y + Z'. X was work, Y was pleasure and Z was being able to shut up! It's fascinating to know that one of the greatest minds of this century thought a third of his success came from his ability to shut up!

So learn to listen and do it easily!

1. **Listen with interest.** Don't just pretend to be interested. Listen eagerly. I have seen many a salesman smile, listen, even look his prospect in the eye and all that time be far away, thinking of anything but what the prospect was saying. If you catch yourself doing this, give up the habit now. Always listen with interest to what prospects have to say. You will always gain something from it!
2. **Do not write down what the prospect tells you.** Listen, but don't write while she is talking. If you do that, it will look as if you have your mind on other things.

3. **Forget your critical thoughts** while the prospect is talking to you. You may think me foolish when I say that negative thoughts show! But they do. And your client could pick them up! Don't say to yourself, 'Oh, what a bore! When will he stop talking?' or 'His office is a mess' or 'How can he wear such an awful suit?' Even if you keep smiling while you are thinking these things, somehow your prospect will register your negative reactions. If you really are getting bored or critical, keep interested by trying to guess what he will say next. I have learned that trick and so can you. It will help you to concentrate!
4. **Do not cut the potential client short.** Listen to her without interrupting. Don't try to add your insight or correct her. I know this is difficult in sales, but you cannot afford to make the prospect feel that you are not interested in what she has to say.
5. **Remember: silence is golden!**

Summary

1. Professional salespeople know the advantages of listening. You will also sell better by listening more and often.
2. Do not *pretend* to listen: do listen!
3. Do not cut your prospect short – ever!

Chapter 17

Be Demonstrative and Enthusiastic

Some time ago a salesman phoned me asking for an appointment. He was going to show me samples of PR and corporate gifts. It is said that professional salespeople make excellent buyers, and so, true to the saying, I agreed to see my caller. Soon after he began his presentation, however, I knew I would not buy from him. He was slow and lacked enthusiasm. He never tuned in to my 'wavelength'.

A sale should be like a good television programme: a good picture with a great sound track. If your television set is not tuned to the proper frequency, you will not get a good reception or pleasant sound. When you select a certain channel and your volume control is not properly set, the sound reception will be poor and the volume might be too high. In sales, if you seem too aggressive or talk too fast or too loud, your client might be tempted to run away. On the other hand, if you are slow or unenthusiastic, you will bore the prospect to death.

Like laughter, enthusiasm is contagious. Your speech and your gestures, as well as your enjoyment of what you are doing, will influence your prospect. Your enthusiasm for your employer, career, product or service will show – through the intonation, pitch and modulation of your voice.

If you show energy, it will give you an irresistible, dynamic quality. It will turn any ordinary presentation into a vigorous proposition. It will stimulate and increase your prospect's interest. Your enthusiasm can turn the prospect's polite acceptance into the desire to act immediately. *Be enthusiastic!* From this date on, be a little *more enthusiastic* every day!

I have always felt that most of the salespeople I have met during my career knew the advantages of enthusiasm. But many didn't use their knowledge to full advantage. Others, because of their own personality, had a tendency to hide their enthusiasm. This leads us to a question: can you become enthusiastic if you are not enthusiastic by nature? My answer is yes. If, early in your profession, you *force* yourself to become enthusiastic, you will soon get into the habit of it!

As you know, early in my selling career I was afraid. Thinking back, I believe I was also a bit shy. It is nearly impossible to show enthusiasm when you are afraid and it is even more difficult to do so when you are timid. But I got over it, mostly because I *wanted to*! My progress was slow. I trained myself to forget my fear and timidity. I did it by thinking of the *advantages* my services could bring to my clients and prospects. By bringing these advantages to my mind constantly, I forced myself to *act* and later to *be* truly *enthusiastic*.

We must also learn to become demonstrative. It is not enough to make gestures or talk with your hands. In our profession, your voice is more important than your hands. You must use it to your advantage. One way of being demonstrative by using your voice is to lower and raise it. Even better, you can accentuate certain words during the presentation. Let your voice show enthusiasm, even when you are answering the simplest of your prospect's questions.

Some time ago, my wife and I went shopping for a portable air conditioner. In the first shop, the salesman simply named the various makes and models, pointing out the prices. When we asked the difference between two quite similar models, the answer was that both units would do the same job but that in one case we would be paying for the name. After a few minutes, the salesman excused himself and started talking to a colleague, leaving us alone. I never buy anything from an uninterested salesperson, so we left and went to another shop.

In the second shop, a pleasant, smiling salesman greeted us and asked us in which room we wanted to install the air conditioner. He explained that this was important because different units had different noise levels. For a bedroom he wouldn't recommend the same model as for a kitchen. Next, he asked about the size of the room, so that he could decide how powerful a unit we needed. Finally, although the model he recommended was slightly more expensive, we bought from him.

What made the difference for us? It was the *demonstrative* answer he gave to my wife's question: 'Is this a safe model as far as the risk of fire is concerned?' I am sure he had not heard this question often, but he replied immediately, without going into lengthy technical detail. He simply said, 'This unit is as safe as the lamp you leave on when you go out at night'. He was an enthusiastic and demonstrative salesperson and, on top of everything else, he was quick off the mark.

Stay sincere while acting with enthusiasm. Emphasise certain words. You remember, I am sure, some of the examples that you received in your early sales instruction. They demonstrated that the same sentence can have a different meaning when different words are emphasised. Here is one example.

Our guarantee protects you for one year

Say this sentence loudly, emphasising the word 'our'. This means, 'You will get a good guarantee from *our* firm, but I don't know what my competitors will offer you'.

Now say the sentence again, emphasising the word 'guarantee'. This means, 'This *guarantee*, Mr James, which is written into the contract. . .'

If you want to tell your prospect that he can sleep peacefully and not worry about his car spending a lot of time in the garage, you would emphasise the word 'protects'.

If you want to point out that the guarantee is for a long time, you would emphasise the phrase 'one year'.

This example can be adapted to your own product or service. As you practise emphasis, you will become more *demonstrative!*

Develop your enthusiasm

May I suggest that you ask yourself the following questions *every day* for the next ten days?

1. **Do I look happy?** This does not mean that you should force yourself to smile all the time. Make your eyes dance and let your natural smile break the ice for you.
2. **Is my voice pleasant?** Do you get the feeling that people who listen to your presentation do it with pleasure? Use a tape recorder to improve the pitch and tone of your voice.
3. **Do I set the volume of my voice at the right level?** Sometimes a deep, quiet voice is more effective than a loud one. A shrill voice is never appealing. Adjust your own volume to the right level.
4. **Is my speech vivacious enough?** You don't have to speak fast or loud to give a lively presentation. One of the best salespeople I know speaks in a very low voice. He speaks so low, in fact, that people have to listen closely and get closer to hear everything he says. He admitted to me that his 'trick' had worked once, and that he has been using it ever since.
5. **Do I look people in the eye?** Your enthusiasm will be transmitted through a direct, intense look.

6. **Is my posture good?** If you let yourself slump in your chair, you'll look dejected and uninterested in your own product or service. Try to bend forward towards your prospect. It will show that you are all ears, and interested.
7. **Is my presentation concise?** We all tend to talk too much, but especially when we are unsure of what we are saying. To maintain your prospect's attention, speak less but always clearly.
8. **Am I a good actor?** To sell better, you should dramatise a bit, without exaggerating. You may laugh, but this is what I do from time to time. When I lose my prospect's attention, I get up from my chair suddenly. Try it. It has a dramatic effect, and it regains my prospect's attention. It never fails!

Summary

1. The enthusiasm you show through words and actions is contagious.
2. To give a dynamic presentation, you must be demonstrative.
3. Being demonstrative doesn't mean talking with your hands. It means being quick on the uptake, anticipating the prospect's questions and being ready with all the necessary information.
4. Raise and lower your voice and accentuate certain words to make your presentation more interesting.
5. A forced smile does not show enthusiasm. Put a sparkle in your eye and the smile will just come naturally.
6. To increase your enthusiasm, ask yourself:

   - Do I look happy?
   - Is my voice pleasant?
   - Do I set the volume of my voice at the right level?

- Is my speech vivacious enough?
- Do I look people in the eye?
- Is my posture good?
- Is my presentation concise?
- Am I a good actor?

Part 4
Sell! Do Not Offer

Chapter 18

Offering, Selling and Pressure Selling

Some time ago, I was at the Mayfair Hotel in London, where I was giving a seminar. I was early, so I sat down in the lobby to wait before going into the seminar room. Not far from where I was sitting, a young man speaking English with a heavy French accent was showing his wine list to a very British-looking gentleman, who, I assumed, was a restaurant owner because he kept saying things like, 'Send me three cases of this one, two cases of that'. The Frenchman was just sitting there flipping the pages of his display book, which contained the labels of the wines he was selling. I was witnessing an 'order taker' at work.

I am sure the young man thought he was selling, but all he was really doing was taking orders. The proprietor of the restaurant needed to fill up his wine cellar, and this salesman happened to have some wines that he wanted. If the salesman had shown a little enthusiasm and drive, he would have sold much more. His boss would have been happier and his commission would have been considerably larger.

Now you be the judge! Who is selling and who is just offering in these examples:

- This machine comes with a five-year guarantee.

or

- You'll save a lot by buying this machine. Some of your competitors already have it. And our latest model is not only guaranteed for five years by the manufacturer but . . .

- All our delivery cars have two-way radio communication.

  or

- We remain at your entire disposal 24 hours a day and we are never farther away than a local phone call. So our express delivery service . . .

- Our travel agency has engaged the best guides for each country on our European tour.

  or

- If you travel with us, you'll have the advantage of our local guide's experience at no extra expense. He will show you around and take you to the most fascinating sights. He knows how to avoid delays and will recommend those small family restaurants that he himself enjoys, in his own city . . .

- Our firm was established in 1891.

  or

- At no extra cost, you will have the advantages of our vast experience. You know, I am sure, that our firm is celebrating its hundredth anniversary this year . . .

- Our special this month covers our 1980 vintage. You will find the price of our white wines . . .

  or

- Your regular clients will be pleasantly surprised to discover that you have expanded your wine list. Our 1980 vintage will give them lots to talk about and they'll be delighted that our special white wine prices apply to it too.

- Laboratory tests show . . .

  or
- Think of the number of patients who will be grateful . . .

- Our delivery schedule is good . . .

  or
- Executives at your company will be pleased to find that we can ship immediately . . .

- We match all our local competitors' prices on these radiators.

  or
- Come hail, snow, ice or rain, your family will be well protected with these radiators . . .

- Our service will allow you to . . .

  or
- From this date on, your staff will be happier and your production will increase in leaps and bounds.

By trying to *sell* your product instead of just *offering* it, you will immediately gain positive reactions from prospective clients. Sales experts vary widely in their methods of doing this. I follow four basic principles which, I believe, can help most salespeople.

1. Discover and use simple key words to sell your product or service.
2. Assume that a favourable decision is being made or will be made at the end of your presentation and that the sale will be closed. Act with confidence!
3. Throughout your presentation keep on asking easy questions to which the prospect has no choice but to answer yes.
4. Ask questions assuming that the sale is closed.

Let's examine each of these principles separately.

Use simple key words

The English language is full of different words that express the same thought. Some are more difficult than others. There are a few that have no appeal to the emotions, but some evoke vivid images and stir the imagination. These are the ones that will keep the prospect alert and waiting to hear more. I have met many salespeople who spoke elegantly but sold little. It is the unsophisticated, direct words that reach the brain faster and seem to trigger reactions. I have never found it useful to sprinkle my presentation with long words.

I'll give you just one example, which you may find elementary, but it has worked for me. See if you can adapt it to your selling field. The salesperson who speaks with elegance but sells little says, 'Sir, our professional management invests your hard-earned capital in the bluest of blue chips. . .' The salesperson who sells a lot says, 'Today, after opening your account, you will become co-owner of some of the best corporations in the world. This means that every time you drive your car, every time you shave, every time you pick up the phone, your money will be working for you. Moreover, every time you throw a used razor blade away, *you will be making money*. Since you are a shareholder, your money will be working for you every time a product is sold.'

Assume that a favourable decision will be made

By going in with the attitude that your prospect will decide to buy your product or service, you will show self-confidence. And self-confidence leads to more sales. Lack of it means disaster. When you believe that your product will help your prospective clients, you will think that they *should* buy it, and your chances of success will increase tremendously. Never confuse self-confidence with overeagerness. Those who do run the risk of pressure selling. Avoid saying things like, 'Should you buy . . .' or 'If you become a client of mine . . .' Instead, say, 'As soon as I fill in your order form in a few minutes . . .' or 'As a client of our firm . . .'

When you assume naturally that the sale is made or will soon be made, you are helping your prospect. Remember, very few people like to be sold to! You will *never* say, 'I suppose that you are all ready to buy my product!' – but this thought will be in your *mind* at all times.

Try to determine the prospect's mood throughout the presentation by asking simple key questions. Her answers will indicate whether everything is going according to plan. If things are not clear in the prospect's mind she will not sign! Therefore, you must ask some key questions *before* the end of your presentation, that is, before it's too late to give more explanations, and you are turned down. Some good salespeople do better: they start filling in the order form, which they keep right next to their notebook. If no immediate objection comes from their prospect, they know that the sale is closed.

Ask questions that invite a yes response

Prepare a number of key questions to which all your prospects must answer positively. As your prospect gets used to saying yes to your questions all along, chances are that he or she is not going to switch to no when the time comes for you to ask for the order.

Here are some examples:

- 'When you leave for a long trip, I am sure you are concerned for your safety and the safety of your family, aren't you?'

- 'You know, don't you, that these tyres will save you petrol?'
- 'As you can see on the order form, you have seven days to change your mind and cancel if you so desire.'

Make up some 'positive-answer' questions that you can use. Personally, I have found it helpful to use questions and phrases such as, 'Don't you think?' and 'I'm sure you would agree that . . .'. By obtaining quick approval on a minor point or observation from my prospects, I have been able to evaluate their thinking and get them on my side.

A good friend of mine, who is one of the top insurance salesmen in the country, owes much of his success to his unwavering enthusiasm. He is so positive in everything he does that he even nods his head up and down every time he asks his prospect a question. It looks as if he is answering yes to his own question. Sure enough, the client says yes too!

If you are tactful, positive and enthusiastic in asking questions like the ones above, you'll get a yes every time.

Questions that will close the sale

Since you are assuming that the order will be yours, you can ask some direct questions to get answers on details such as delivery dates, method of payment, address, etc. When you get these answers, you will know automatically that the sale is concluded. For example, you might ask:

- 'Is this order to be charged to your personal account or to the company's?'
- 'Do you require this material next week or will a three-week delivery be acceptable?'
- 'Is sea freight acceptable or do you require air shipment?'
- 'Is a first shipment of ten dozen cases acceptable or do you require the entire 30 dozen at once?'

- 'I assume that you do want your children included among the beneficiaries of your policy.'
- 'Would you prefer to give me a cheque now or would you rather pay on delivery?'

Have you noticed? Whatever the answer, your prospect has automatically indicated willingness to buy. Prepare some questions of your own, adapted to your product or service, and use them tomorrow with your first prospect. They will help your sales.

Do you remember the gold pens that my Lebanese salesman friend gives his clients? When he hands over his pen to the prospect at the end of his presentation and says, 'Would you prefer to use my pen or yours?' he is drawing out a positive reaction from his client. If the client answers, 'Yours', he is in fact stating, 'I am buying!' And if he answers, 'Mine', he is also buying!

I have often used one of the following questions:

- 'What is your middle initial, Mr Hughes?'
- 'Your surname is spelled with two n's, is it not?'
- 'Should we post this to your home address or to your office?'
- 'This is number 120 High Street, is it not?'

When my client gives me the answer to any of the above, I calmly copy it down on the order pad, because I am *assuming*, and rightly so, that my sale is closed. If the order requires his signature, I simply hand my client the form and say, 'Would you kindly put your OK on this line and check the address to make sure I didn't forget anything?'

As it is very natural to sign a purchase order, not many object to signing it. Some, however, could say, 'Wait a minute, I haven't told you I was buying!' It has happened to me and it will happen to you too, but remember, it is much less likely to happen than if you say, 'Would you agree,

Mr Johnson, to give me your order today?' or 'Which model would you prefer?' or 'Have you decided whether you want to have this machine installed?' or, simply, 'What do you think?'

The professional method of closing a sale that I have just described applies to a shop situation as well. In that case, too, you should always draw out a positive reaction from your clients. You should not forget that they came into the shop with the intention of buying. You could ask questions like 'Should I have it delivered in the morning or the afternoon?' or 'Shall I have it gift-wrapped for you now?' or 'Can we step into my office? I am sending your new car to the service area to have everything checked. You'll be able to leave with your lovely new car tomorrow evening'.

Don't use words that give your prospects a cold shower. Use words that warm their hearts! And ask them questions that make them say yes!

Pressure selling is unprofessional

By instinct we all resist pressure, but we all do it in different ways. If I started to push you around, you might push me back or simply resist. But one thing is certain, none of us likes to be pressured.

In our profession, if you make the mistake of pressuring your prospect or client, you end up being the loser. Never be aggressive. Learn to be unpretentious, straightforward and courteous. At the same time, you must never forget that you are selling.

Never be too anxious either. You will run the risk of wanting to interrupt your prospect too often.

Remember that your profession is to sell. Explain this to your prospect without being aggressive. The person you are facing knows that you are a salesman. Don't be shy to say so and show it!

If you observe the best professionals in our business, you will notice that they are calm but resolute. Don't try to speak too smoothly. Do it in a polite and gracious manner, but always aim to close the sale.

Never become a teacher! Professors teach, they *do not sell*! It won't help you to go into minute details. This will not make your prospect want to buy your product or service. You must *sell* to the potential client by giving him or her the urge to buy. Products and services are never bought; they are sold. You will never succeed in getting the prospect in the buying mood by submerging the poor person with technical explanations.

Summary

1. It's nice to offer, but it's nicer to sell!
2. Drawing out a positive reaction is called 'selling'.
3. Use simple, unsophisticated words in your presentation.
4. Be positive and self-confident. Assume from the start that the sale will be closed.
5. Ask your prospect simple questions throughout the interview that evoke a yes response.
6. Ask your prospect questions about delivery arrangements and name spellings, and fill in the order form with this information as you speak. Then just ask your client to sign the order form.
7. Forget for ever phrases like 'Well, what do you think?' and 'So, would you be interested in buying?'
8. By instinct, we all tend to resist pressure.
9. Never push anyone into buying. Stay calm, polite and courteous.
10. Never become a teacher while selling.

Chapter 19

The Progressive Sale

One response leads to the next

Many years ago, I watched with fascination as an evangelist on Canadian television made what I have since come to call the 'progressive sale'. He was preaching to an audience of several thousand. At one point, in the course of his sermon, he asked those who wanted him to pray for them to raise their hands. Hundreds of hands rose. 'Higher', he said, and everyone obeyed. As he started praying, his helpers moved to stand at the end of each row where hands had been raised. When he asked these people to follow his helpers down the aisle to join him, most came.

What had happened was a progressive sale. Had the evangelist simply asked members of his congregation to 'Come on down the aisle to join him', few would have done so! Instead, he proceeded step by step – *progressively*! He first asked people to raise their hands, then had them raise them higher, and finally asked them to get up. It was easy, then, for the people to follow his helpers and come forward.

You can adapt the progressive method to your type of selling. All you have to do is use some of the key questions I have always used, or make up your own. They should help you as much as mine have helped me.

(a) You would want your car to give you a comfortable ride, wouldn't you, Mr Phillips?
(b) Added to a comfortable ride, you would want it to be the *safest* ride available, wouldn't you?
(c) Added to comfort and safety, you would want your car to look good and your tyre replacements to be reasonable in price, I am sure, wouldn't you?

Agree with your prospect

Another way of letting your prospect progress gradually to the position of making a purchase is to agree with a statement he or she has made. It is a very successful method. You might say, 'I totally agree with you when you state that . . .'; or, 'I fully understand that you would prefer dealing with a close friend. However, the advantage of our firm is that it regards *all* of its clients as friends. This is what I do, too'; or, 'You said a moment ago that you would prefer a four-door model. Here's one in . . .'

Small or large, make the sale

Many of my colleagues insist on trying for the *big* sale. They feel that their time is wasted on a small one. I have often experienced the opposite, and have gained a lot of satisfaction from starting a small scheme for a prospect who became a friend thereafter. When I went back to my client for the after-sale servicing, the door opened easily. The 'client-salesperson' relationship had been established. I was no longer seeing a prospect. He had become a client, and trust and respect had been established. So if you are unable to close a large sale, try for a smaller one.

A trainee once requested my help. He had been unable to

open an account for a prospect who had invested heavily with a competitor. I met the prospect with him. This is a summary of our conversation.

'I know, Mr Robinson, that I will never be able to convince you to transfer your investment, and I am not going to try. However, having heard a lot about you, I also know that if I proposed an interesting little game today that would pose little risk, you wouldn't be against it, would you?'

'Maybe not', he answered.

'This is what I propose. I am going to open a *minimum* account for you. It will take only one-hundredth of your present investment with my colleague. That isn't much, is it?'

'No', he agreed.

'Having become a client of our firm, I'm sure you'll try to outwit our investment experts. As our client, you will receive a statement showing the results of your portfolio every quarter. If you find that our experts are doing better than you are doing on your own, you might decide to increase your account with us *without my being here to influence your decision*. If, on the other hand, you outwit our experts, it will not take long to close the small account I am going to open for you now. I suppose that you would prefer to receive your documents at your home address, would you not? What is your exact address, please?'

It was an easy close from then on.

Our trainee did not know it at the time, but he was instrumental in helping to open the account of our firm's largest client ever. His commission was small to start with, but later he made a bundle!

I recommend the above method to all salespeople. Try to open as many client accounts as possible. It doesn't matter if they are small at the beginning. They will grow, and so will your earnings!

Summary

1. Using the progressive method, it is easier to get approval all along, including the final yes response.
2. Quote your prospects! Agree with them! They'll like it.
3. Do not push for large sales all the time. By gaining a small client today, your earnings will grow with the account.

Chapter 20

It Pays to Help Your Prospects

I once accompanied a trainee to an appointment with a prospect he was having difficulty selling a savings scheme to. The man was a restaurant owner, and while we were sitting having a discussion the prospect watched his employees, often getting up to greet customers or help out. Needless to say, we couldn't keep his attention for long. I was on the verge of suggesting an after-hours meeting when his wife arrived. She started to look after things in the restaurant, and he relaxed. So did we.

Our prospect proved to be a difficult one. He kept saying no. I was in a spot. It was against my nature to insist, but on the other hand, I had to prove to my young trainee that nothing was impossible. So I did insist and the prospect kept saying no. Finally, after two hours, we left with a signed document and a cheque to open up the savings scheme.

Early the next day, I was not too surprised when my secretary informed me that our client's wife was on the phone. I knew I had pushed too hard and thought she wanted to cancel the arrangement. I was greatly surprised when the woman said, 'I waited for my husband to leave the house this morning so I could call you and thank you. You will never know how much you have helped me and my son. My husband would never admit it, but he is a gambler!

Because of that, we have no savings. Now at least I know that my son's education will be provided for and I can stop worrying. You can rest assured that I will religiously send our cheque to your bank every month. Thanks again.'

My trainee was not the only one who learned from this experience. It confirmed two facts in my mind. First, that you should not always believe the reasons your prospects give for not wanting to buy. They are often untrue! Second, in our profession, we are often helping people without knowing it and more than we realise.

You can also help your prospects in other ways. If the occasion arises, don't miss out! One of my better salespeople once described his nicest sale. A client told him that he should go to see his rich uncle, a farmer. The presentation was fairly short: the uncle had urgent things to do. He was not interested in a savings scheme. In fact, he left the kitchen table before my salesman had time to pick up his papers.

When he walked to his car, which was parked in the yard, he noticed that the uncle was working under the hood of a large tractor. He approached and offered to help out, explaining that diesel engines were his hobby. Dropping his jacket and rolling up his sleeves, he worked and worked and solved the farmer's problem by that evening. He was pleasantly surprised to be invited back to the house for a drink, and it wasn't long before the farmer's wife asked him to stay for supper. By the time he left, he had been asked to return the next day because, on second thoughts, the idea of a savings scheme wasn't all that silly. . . The next day, my salesman could not conceal his surprise as he counted a tall stack of damp pound notes that were to be used to open the account. He never knew whether those bills came from the attic or one of the outhouses.

Do you believe me when I say that our salesman was trusted because of the spontaneous help he'd offered the farmer? *Be helpful! You will leave the competition behind.*

Today, many products are similar. Why do you prefer one petrol station to another? Why did you open your bank account at this local bank instead of another? What made you choose your insurance company over its competitors? Generally speaking, if we are 'looked after' or given good service, we are satisfied. As a professional salesperson, be obliging and willing to help. You will never be sorry!

Some time ago, a print shop representative came to call on us. When I asked why we should buy our supplies from him he said, 'When you purchase from us, you are also acquiring my services. I am sure that I can be of help!' He is now our regular supplier.

In my opinion, there is only one way to surpass your competitors: you must always *do your very best* and be as helpful as possible. Do it sincerely and do not hold back. Experience will show you that when you learn to *give*, sales will come your way regardless of price or other factors.

Serious technical salespeople always send new and useful information to their clients. This is one way of being helpful. Others do it to stay in touch. You know that people tend to buy again from professionals who keep in touch and keep their clients informed about new techniques related to their machines or products. They will certainly be reluctant to buy again from salespeople who dropped out of sight after their first sale.

Recently, some friends of ours wanted to build a swimming pool in their garden. They asked for several estimates, but finally settled for the company that promised excellent after-sales service. They never saw their salesman again after they signed up. As a result, they changed suppliers and told all their friends about the lack of service from the outfit that had built their beautiful pool.

Never forget to deliver what you have promised! *After-sales servicing* is essential in whatever line of products or services you are working.

If you are working in the financial or insurance area, you can sometimes ask an older client, 'What is the exact amount of your retirement income?' You will be surprised to discover that many do not know! By helping them to calculate it, you will be lending a helping hand. Some insurance companies also offer free analysis of their clients' policies. This can often be a great help.

Take the initiative! Help people by asking questions.

If you help your clients today, you'll receive orders in the future.

Summary

1. Help your prospect by leading him to a positive decision.
2. The help you give will come back to you in the form of orders.
3. Spontaneous help will establish a good relationship between you and the prospect or client.
4. An obliging salesperson will leave the competition behind.
5. Always try to do your best.
6. Deliver what you promised! Make sure the after-sales servicing is carried out.
7. Give good service and oblige, and you'll hear less and less about competitors.

Chapter 21

Put Yourself in Your Prospect's Shoes

Have you ever asked yourself whether you would buy if you were in your prospect's shoes? This little question can often help you to answer questions your prospects may have. Once or twice in my selling career, I had to find the strength *not* to sell my product to certain clients. During the course of my presentation, I realised that they had financial obligations that meant they should not buy. On these occasions, my common sense was strong enough to keep me from selling to them. But I was a winner all the same because of the referrals I received from the prospects I lost.

How do you climb into your prospect's shoes?

It's one thing to say that you should put yourself in your client's shoes. It's quite another to do it. When I was first selling, I often asked myself how to go about it. Then I remembered the estate agent who sold us our first house. This man was well organised. Before anyone had ever heard of multiple listings, he kept cards for every property he had in his portfolio. On these, he listed all the information you ever wanted or needed, including local schools, shops, parks, libraries, churches, and many details about the property itself. It would be silly for an estate agent to keep cards like this today, but let me tell you that at that time this agent was the 'super organiser'. I was so impressed by the wealth of information he had to show us that I decided to adapt his system to our financial services. This marvellous system was one of the keys to my success in selling. It also helped me to put myself in my prospect's shoes.

When I could not close a sale after giving a presentation, I would go home and write up a 'prospect card' describing the person I had just left. I made sure to include all the information he had given me while it was still fresh in my mind. When I returned for my second visit, the prospect was very impressed because I remembered so much about him, his family, his business, his investments and his insurance policies. I knew then, as I know now, that these little 'secret' cards were responsible for 70 per cent of the sales I closed on a second call. I would be able to put all my prospects' data in front of them, and I would simply say, 'Mrs Fairbank, if I were in your shoes, this is what I would do'. In most cases, since my proposal was logical, prospects would agree and the sale would be closed.

The cards, in fact, became mini-files. I had them printed so that I would only have to fill in the blanks when I left my prospect's office or home. Later, as an added personal financial service, I even carried with me a printed sample of a Last Will and Testament, which I left with clients who had need for it.

Some professionals say, 'Mr Price, if I were in your shoes, do you know what I would do?' Invariably the prospect asks, 'What would you do?' By asking this, the prospect is in fact seeking help in making a decision. The salesperson can give a concise résumé of the situation and conclude the sale with all kinds of positive reasons for buying now.

I have known others who say, 'Mr Wilson, I am trying to

put myself in your shoes to determine what I would do in your position. To be able to give you unbiased advice, I need more personal information.' After listening to the prospect give more information, they would simply say, 'In this case, this is what I recommend . . .' or 'This is what I would do'.

Referring to other clients

You can also put yourself in the other person's shoes by referring to other clients. (In a way, you are saying that these are people you would consult if you were in your prospect's position.) If your prospect says, 'Is there really a saving in the long run if I buy such an expensive machine now?' it is fairly easy to demonstrate that other clients have not only saved money but have also made profits by buying early.

A prospect might say, 'You mention your excellent after-sales service. How do I know it's really that good?' Here again, by referring to other satisfied clients, it is easy to close the sale. You could say, 'Mr Stead had the same reservation before he became a client. I know that he is perfectly happy with our product. He told me so only last week.'

This method can be used by people selling many different kinds of things. However, it is unthinkable to use it for financial products and services. In this case, clients' names must be kept strictly confidential unless they have already given approval for their use.

Summary

1. Ask yourself, 'Why would I buy this product or service?' Put yourself in your prospect's shoes.
2. Give unbiased advice once you have looked at things from the prospect's perspective as well as your own.
3. Gather all the pertinent data about your prospect.

4. To convince people professionally, say, 'This is what I would do'.
5. Depending on the product or service you are selling, you may be able to refer to other satisfied clients to help close a sale.
6. Always ask clients' permission before referring to them as satisfied customers.

Part 5

Closing the Sale Means Asking for the Cheque

Chapter 22

How Are You Going to Make that Sale?

Solicit the order

Most salespeople know how to do everything well except to *ask for the order*! Asking for the order is not pressure selling. Many sales are lost simply because the salesperson didn't know how to ask for the order or didn't have the nerve to do it. But if you don't ask for the order, there can never be a sale!

Many hesitate; others simply freeze when the 'moment' comes. They hope and pray that the prospect is going to say, 'All right, I am going to buy from you. Give me a red one'. They know they have presented the right information and they know they have answered the prospect's first objection. So they wait . . . and they wait! *They wait for the prospect to buy!* Statistics prove that nine times out of ten prospects do *not* buy. They have to be sold!

Methods of closing a sale depend on the product or service sold, but also on the temperament and personality of the salesperson. However, one method is essential for everyone: *you have to ask for the order and the cheque*.

Here's an example. 'You are asking if this lawnmower can do the same job as your neighbour's? Mr Butterwell, your new mower will do a faster job because it has a larger engine and it is self-propelled. Can we deliver this Saturday or would you prefer to pick it up yourself from our warehouse?'

I have met many salespeople who are very much at ease when the time comes to close the sale. They are usually very calm and act professionally. Others can be just gauche: they are tactless and awkward. They seem to be begging for the order. When this happens, both the prospect and the salesperson are ill at ease, and the sale is in jeopardy.

Adapt yourself to each client and situation, but remember: you must always solicit the order! If you don't, your client will not consider you a professional. Good salespeople ask for the order. If you want to be considered, you have to ask!

Take the order form out at the beginning

When I started selling, no one had ever explained to me that it would help me greatly if I took the order form out of my briefcase at the beginning of the interview. As I went along, however, I noticed that when I reached for my order pad at the time of closing the sale, my prospects would make some kind of backward movement. Some would even state, 'Wait a minute. What is that? I'm not ready to buy! I have to look at this closely. . .'

Of course, the order form was new to the prospect. He or she had never seen it before and had to read it. Once prospects got over the initial shock, they would ask, 'Why all these questions? What is that? Why do you want to know this? My solicitor will have to go through this. . .'

I learned to take the order form out as soon as I began the presentation. I used it to point out the answers to certain questions or to explain some advantages. I would purposely show where those were listed on the order. This gave many people confidence. The order form gradually became part of the presentation. Then no one seemed surprised when I started filling in the blanks at 'closing time'!

When I describe this method to some salespeople during seminars, I often hear objections. They say, 'Surely this is pressure selling. We couldn't do that.' I have only one answer to this objection: if you follow my advice, your sales will increase by at least 25 per cent! Pulling your order pad out at the beginning of the presentation is not pressure selling – it is a professional way of selling.

Close early and at all times

At the beginning of their careers, most salespeople have a tendency to close the sale at the end of the presentation. They have been taught to sell that way. Experienced professionals, on the other hand, try to close the sale early. 'How early?', I can hear you ask. 'Earlier than you thought possible' is my answer.

Let me explain. You should learn to be ready to close the sale at any time. You should not wait for a specific moment. And you must try to close as early as possible.

For example, you might say, 'This type of heater can save you enough money to pay for one month's electricity per year. I am sure that a 10 per cent saving would be of interest to your family, Mrs Woodbridge, would it not?' You've made only one point in your presentation, but you have already tried to close the sale. Mrs Woodbridge may be ready to buy at this point if the 10 per cent saving is important to her.

Here are two more examples of 'early-closing' statements:

'Now that you see the great savings this new central heating system will give you, you will want to replace your windows.' You have met an objection by pointing out the savings, and you are trying to close the sale.

'This apartment has a magnificent view over the bay and it's large enough to have your children and friends to stay from time to time, but the maintenance is minimal. I assume you would be interested in the mortgage details. Let's sit here and review the application.' You are trying to close after a short visit to the property.

There are many important moments to watch for when you are trying to close a sale. Sometimes the prospect is indicating that he or she is ready to buy. These tiny 'buying signals' are difficult to pick up when you are learning. Experience, and *only* experience, will let you catch on to them before the moment passes. A simple physical gesture such as leaning forward slightly will indicate 'I am ready to buy!'

When you hear, feel or see such a signal, you must *stop your presentation and try to close the sale immediately*. Do not wait! That's what you're there for. You know it and your prospect knows it. Say simply, 'I know you made the right decision' or 'In the years to come, you will be very happy with your . . .!' That's it. Be happy and go. The sale has been made. The prospect likes your product and has bought it.

Here are a few examples of buying signals:

- 'Yes, I suppose it is a good deal, but . . .'
- 'Yes, I was going to get one this month, but the extra expenses I had to face . . .'
- 'I think it would be wise to wait a little while . . .'
- 'I think it is a little too expensive for us at the moment . . .'

Most inexperienced salespeople would think that the above replies are *objections*. They are not! They are buying signals. The professional will simply reassure the prospect: if he buys now, it will be a safe and profitable investment. In many instances, that's all it takes! And the sale is concluded.

If you don't try, you won't succeed. This short sentence is important. You must try to close often and early. Do not fail to distinguish between an objection and a buying signal. Often the difference between the two is slight. It could be one little word or simply the tone of voice. If the phrase includes 'I think', 'I suppose', 'I believe', 'I should', 'I shouldn't', it is a *signal* and not an *objection.* In any case, what can go wrong if you try to close at the wrong time? Your prospect can say no, which really means that she is *not yet ready to buy*.

Perhaps you haven't given her enough details about your equipment or the financial advantages of your product. Perhaps you should continue with your presentation and go into details on some particular point she mentioned. A little later, try closing your sale again!

Tomorrow, try closing much sooner than you have ever done in previous presentations. As professional salespeople we tend to forget that at times we can bore our prospects with a long presentation. In fact, we are probably boring on many occasions. Suppose that your product is well advertised or well known. Then a long presentation is not necessary. So why not close earlier? Try it! You will be amazed at the success you have – starting tomorrow! If you don't succeed on your first try, continue a little further and *try again!*

When I teach this method in my seminars or classes, I am often told, 'But my prospect will not know all the advantages of my product (or service) if I do not reach the end of my presentation. I have to tell him everything!' I agree. You *must!* But, please, *do it on another day!* Close the sale first and then come back and explain everything. Your new *client* will be happy to see you again and hear all the things you had no time to tell him when he was only a *prospect*.

You could say, for example, 'Mr Murray, your new purchase offers other advantages. I will explain them all, once you have taken delivery next week. Would Tuesday. . .?'

By trying to close early, you:

- save time: yours and your prospect's;
- can close a sale without running the risk of saying too much and losing it;
- have several occasions to close – if you wait for the end of your presentation, you only have one opportunity to close;
- eliminate the risk of making a big case out of a small sale;
- gain respect – you act like a professional; you sell better and more easily than others.

Summary

1. Asking for the order is not pressure selling.
2. All products and services are sold. Few are bought.
3. Adapt yourself to each prospect and situation to close the sale.
4. Show your prospect the order form right at the beginning of your presentation.
5. Try to close early, or earlier than you usually do.
6. Learn to notice buying signals.
7. Distinguish between objections and buying signals.
8. Try to close after you have:

    - made a point
    - crossed a hurdle
    - noticed a buying signal
    - ended your presentation.

9. By closing early you gain respect, time and several opportunities to close. You also eliminate the risk of losing the sale.

Chapter 23
Stop Talking

If you are able to master the following methods, you will be very successful – extremely successful! But beware! It is difficult – very difficult! Some of you will not be able to do it. I know! I have been teaching this method for over 20 years. Only the best, the *very best* will master it, and to do so, they will need a lot of practice.

Well, this is how it works.

At the end of your presentation, you ask your prospect one of your favourite closing questions. Once you have asked it, you *stop talking!* You don't say another word! *Not one word!* And the silence starts. You wait in *total silence . . .*

The silence can last 20 seconds or five minutes. Still, you *do not say one single word! Total silence.* You relax in your chair and wait. It is a silent wait. And it is a *long, silent wait.* It seems longer every second . . . And here you are asking yourself, 'What is he going to say?' And you keep on waiting in total silence. It is difficult, believe me!

Now, here comes the most important part. The person who speaks first has lost. If you happen to utter one single word, if you add anything to your closing questions, if you can't stand the silence any longer and ask another question or even repeat the last question, *you have lost the sale!* You might as well pack up and go home.

If your prospect speaks first, for whatever reason, he will buy your product or service. It seldom fails! I have seen it happen time and time again.

Newcomers and trainees will have great difficulty adjusting to this unusual method of closing sales. In general, they are *afraid of the silence*. They feel – and you will too – that the silence is a tremendous pressure-bearing closing method. But you cannot call it pressure selling. You are not saying a single word! The silence is doing the selling for you! If you think you are strong enough to try this method, please do! You will not be disappointed.

In my selling days, I have experienced only one failure. I was sitting next to my prospect, an electrical engineer. I had concluded my presentation and had asked one of my 'key' closing questions. I then stopped talking and waited for his answer. I relaxed against the back of my chair. The silence was absolute.

You could hear the clock ticking on his desk . . . *silence* . . . I lit a small cigar . . . *more silence* . . . I was waiting . . . It was getting on my nerves. Still, I waited. Not a word.

Suddenly my prospect got up, still silent, walked around his desk and left his office. I waited half an hour, but he didn't come back! I then realised that he knew the method. He knew that if he had said anything, he would probably have bought. So he decided to leave me and my silence . . . I can see you smiling! It is the truth!

Please do me a favour. Try the method yourself tomorrow. But remember: the rule is absolute. If you speak first, you have lost the sale.

As I said before, you will need practice. You will also have to learn *when* to stop talking. Usually it should be after a key question. Let us review a few of these:

- 'I suppose that you would like to receive your documents at home rather than at the office? What is your home address, Mr York?'
- 'I assume that you would like to have delivery before the end of the week, Mrs West. What is your exact home address, please?'
- 'I assume that for the little extra sum of £–, you would prefer the double indemnity clause. What is your home address, Mr. Smith?'
- 'Mrs Whiting will be your first beneficiary, I assume. What is her first name, please?'
- 'I can see that you prefer this set in mahogany. You would want it delivered before the 15th, I am sure. What is your home address, please?'
- 'Your preference would be to lease for tax purposes, I am sure. What is your first name, please?'

To succeed in this type of selling, you must *never stop talking* after a common question. In any case, common questions should be avoided altogether at closing time. Here are three examples of common questions:

- 'What do you think, Mr Jacobs?'
- 'Do you follow?'
- 'Do you like this one?'

I can never say it often enough: it is difficult, but nearly infallible. *Try it.* You will sometimes encounter prospects who will get up from their desks when the silence becomes difficult to live with. *Do not move! Do not say a word! Wait!* Stay cool, calm. At other times, your prospect will start calculating or scribbling on a sheet of paper. Wait! And *do not say anything!*

Remember: let your prospect break the silence. You will be the winner.

When I started using this method, it was still largely unknown, but since this book has been published in French and Spanish, I have heard from many readers in other countries that the method works in other languages too. No wonder: silence is universal. Let me hear from you when you start using it.

Summary

1. At the end of a presentation or demonstration or after having asked a key question, *stop talking*.
2. Wait in total silence.
3. If you speak first, you have probably lost the sale.
4. If you add anything to your last question, you will probably lose the sale.
5. If your prospect speaks first, he or she will probably buy your product or service.
6. The silent method is very difficult, but if you master it, you will have great success with it.

Chapter 24

Never Argue . . . the Client Is Always Right!

Does it pay to win the argument?

Have you ever met a salesperson who has never lost his temper or her composure? I doubt it! Everyone gets upset at times! The professional knows, however, that you always have to discipline yourself to control your emotions when you are facing a prospect or client. If you are unable to control your temper or if you keep on arguing during a presentation, your bank account is going to suffer!

It is never easy to keep calm and not say much, and it's even more difficult to do this when the client is obviously wrong. However, you must get used to it. In all my years of selling, I have come up with only one solution to the problem. When I am on the verge of losing my cool, I try to look at things from the point of view of the prospect. Doing this permits me to make an all-out effort to remain calm. The well-known saying, 'The customer is always right', has always helped me to regain my composure and avoid conflicts with anyone.

The professional salesperson cannot afford to be angry with people. If he starts to argue, will he be the winner? Can she afford to be proud of winning an argument? It's a costly thing to be right and in the process lose a sale!

Never make fun of clients or prospects. Respect their beliefs and their origins. Never arouse ill feelings, never show hostility. Never give advice on private matters or personal situations. As a salesperson, you have *too much to lose*!

How to face an argumentative prospect

It's not easy to do this. You will need patience and experience. But patience can be learned, just like everything else.

This is what I have learned to do when I feel that my prospect wants to argue. I simply turn his arguments around and use them to my advantage. I try to close my sale with his objections.

You can also make an effort to impart your own ideas to her and make her believe that these are really her own! 'Certainly, Ms Parker, many people think as you do. You have put your finger on the most important reason for . . .' and continue by emphasising your own ideas. Never, but *never*, reply to something she states by saying, 'No, Ms Parker, I do not agree' or 'No, Ms Parker, you are wrong'.

Drop the word 'No' from your vocabulary

If only one thing stays in your mind from this chapter, it should be this: *Eliminate for ever the word 'no' from your sales talk and replace it with two words*: 'Yes, but . . .' This is a clever way to increase your chances of selling your products or services. To help you remember to do this, let me give you an exaggerated example. Suppose that a prospect told you one day, 'Look, the moon has turned *green* tonight!' What you do is take a step towards the window, look outside and, turning to face him again, say with your usual smile, '*You are right*, Mr Hastings, but aren't you a little colour-blind at night?'

Summary

1. The client is always right.
2. Never try to win an argument. Even if you win, you'll lose the sale.
3. Never arouse anyone's hostility and never show hostility in a selling situation.
4. Pass along your ideas and make the prospect think they are his or hers.
5. Eliminate for ever the word 'no' and replace it with 'yes, but'.

Chapter 25

Use the Prospect's Objections to Close the Sale

When your prospect *does not have any objections*, beware! You are facing your most difficult closing challenge.

Most trainees dread objections. This is because they are afraid of not being able to find convincing arguments to counter them. In some cases, it is true that you have to find a convincing argument. We will look at a few examples of these in a moment. However, in most cases, I prefer to use my client's objection and turn it around in order to close the sale.

In my early selling days, when I was told, 'Mr Auer, I do not think that your model is as efficient as your competitor's', I had the urge to reply that the efficiency of my machine was tremendous, that it could not be compared to XYZ Corporation's model, that theirs was certainly good but ours was much better . . .

Today I reply, 'Mr Jackson, do I understand your statement correctly? If I could prove to you, *without any doubt whatsoever*, that my machine is as efficient, if not more efficient, than my competitor's, you *would be prepared to give me your order now*. Am I right?' Can you see why he has to answer *yes* to this question? I have taken *his* objection and turned it around. He cannot say no.

All I have to do now is to prove without doubt that my machine is as efficient as my competitor's, and the sale is closed. Since I have been taught how to demonstrate that efficiency, all I have to do after proving it at the end of my demonstration is to fill in my order form. *He cannot object* to that, he told me so a moment earlier when he answered yes. This is how I close sales.

Let's look at a few more examples.

Objection. 'The style of your samples is too avant-garde for our clientele.'
Answer. 'If I understand you correctly, Mr Price, you would like to buy our collection if I could convince you that our style is very much "in" even for your clientele. Isn't that so?'

Again, he has to say yes. He has no other choice! I am using his objection. So all I have to do is show him that our style is very much in fashion, that his competitors know it, that he might be left behind if he does not offer these new styles to his clients, that fashion shows and magazines prove that our avant-garde style is today's choice.

Objection. 'I am sorry, Mr Auer, but I am not interested in an investment scheme without guarantees.'
Answer. 'If I understand correctly, Ms Baker, if I can show you that our schemes are guaranteed, you would be prepared to open your account today. Isn't that so?'

Ms Baker has to say yes in any case, because she doesn't really believe that my schemes do carry guarantees. It is now up to me to explain the various ways we guarantee the income, the capital, the insurance portion, etc. After this convincing evidence, she cannot back out. She said beforehand that she would buy if . . .! So I start filling in the application form.

Whatever your service or product is, try to repeat your prospect's objection. Once he has answered yes, he can hardly retract his previous statement!

However, before using this method, you must learn to determine if the objection given is a *true* one, a *valid* one! You will often find that first objections are rarely true ones. They are given to put you off. Starting tomorrow, try to unmask *fake objections* such as,

- 'I am sorry. I do not need one now.'
- 'I can't afford it now.'
- 'Why don't you come back next week or when you are in the neighbourhood?'
- 'Maybe next month, but now I can't.'

Objections like these are not real ones. They are given to get rid of you. Your prospect is not telling the truth. You must find out what the *true objection* is!

Once you find it, *use it to close the sale.*

Like many other salespeople, I believe that there are seven categories of true objection. They are:

1. price
2. quality of product (or manufacturer's good name)
3. blockade
4. lack of credit or money
5. objections to service or guarantee
6. friendship or reciprocity
7. other objections.

We won't be able to cover all the possible objections here because of the different products and services sold, but a few examples should help you in your line of selling. First, let's review the rules.

1. **Use the prospect's objection to close the sale** (as explained above).
2. **Avoid answering the objection directly**. If you get into that bad habit, you will get drawn into playing 'ping-pong' with the prospect. You get an objection and you

answer. You get another objection and you answer again! Objection-answer. Objection-answer. Objection-answer. Ping-pong is a nice sport, but playing ping-pong with objections is fatal in the selling game. *Avoid it at all costs!*

3. **Discover the true objection**.
4. **A true objection often indicates lack of conviction in the prospect's mind**. You must therefore start your presentation over again, at least in part, to explain further and convince the prospect.
5. **Show your prospect that you welcome her objection.** This is essential! Tell her you are glad and show her your pleasure. She will feel important.
6. **Never ignore or sidestep an objection.** Many experts disagree with me on this subject, but I find my method works best. I'll let you decide! If you get an objection in the middle of your presentation, you could say, 'I am glad, Mr North, to hear you say that. However, if you allow me to go on, I think you will be satisfied with my explanation of this subject in the course of my presentation. I am making a note of it here in case I forget, so that we can come back to it later.' Then *do mark down the objection in large letters* on your worksheet, so that you can use it at the end to *close your sale!*

Types of objection

1. Price

- 'Your price is much too high!' You are going to hear this objection over and over again, whatever it is you are selling. You'll get it in different forms, phrases and sentences. In general, it means that the client wants to be reassured that the product he or she needs to buy is worth the price. You must therefore *emphasise the value* of the purchase.

Better still, you could say, 'Did I understand you correctly, Mr Simmonds? If I can show you that my product is less expensive than my competitor's, you would be ready to buy from me now! Isn't that so?'

- 'Would I really save money if I buy your products?' (She thinks they are too expensive.) You can answer this question as above, with further details about better service, exchange potential, slower deterioration, fewer repairs, etc.

2. Quality of product (or manufacturer's good name)

- 'I had one of your earlier models and was never satisfied with it.' Avoid talking about the past. Concentrate on the present! Say, 'Am I to understand, Mr Bradshaw, that if I could prove to you that our newest model meets your specifications, and that it has been improved tremendously, you would give me your order today?'
- 'I have never heard of your corporation.' To this, you should say, 'Mr Kent, I am sure that you would purchase this item today if I could convince you of (1) the good name of our corporation, (2) the quality of our management, (3) our excellent after-sales service – would you not?'

3. Blockade

- 'Let me think about it.' You must always agree! 'Of course, Mr Fielding, you *must* think about it. This is exactly what my client from the High Street said to me yesterday. However, his business partner who was present remarked, "What do you think you can learn tomorrow that you don't know today?" I think, Mr Fielding, that the partner's idea is valid. What is it that you would want to think about? Is there a point, perhaps, about which you need more explanation? Would you like me to go over it again?'

- 'I must talk to my wife about this.' Again, you must agree. The husband has to consult his wife! Try to make an immediate appointment for you to see them together in the evening of the same day! If he would prefer to discuss the matter with her alone, explain that you are the expert, that you have all the data that he or his wife could ask about, that you can demonstrate the product, etc. You must do your utmost to see them together.

  When faced with this objection, I have often used the following personal technique. With a big smile, I explain that husbands should never teach their wives how to drive. With a bit of theatrics, I have often added this: 'Only yesterday, Mr Morrison, one of my clients mentioned that on the day I gave him a presentation, he went home and told his wife, "Darling, this morning at the office, I met a charming account executive and . . ." "Oh, no," cried his charming wife, "No way! No money, no investments, nothing! And to think that last month you refused the request I made . . ." I know, Mr Morrison, that *your* wife would certainly not react in this silly way, but don't you agree that it would be better if I explained to her, with you at my side, all the interesting features of this scheme? Would 8.30 pm be convenient or would you prefer 9 pm?'

4. Lack of credit or money

- 'I don't have any money at the moment.' When you hear this objection, you should respond, 'If I understand you correctly, Mr Manning, it is only a question of budget. In other words, if you had the money today, you would buy this scheme, wouldn't you?'

  If you are convinced that this is a true objection – in most cases it isn't! – try demonstrating the savings realised by buying immediately. Delays mean loss of potential profit and are often very costly (more so if you are selling life insurance!).

If you sell machinery, you must convince your prospect that it is often more expensive to continue operating with an old machine than to finance a new, better and faster one.

5. Objections to service or guarantee

- 'Your competitors are offering a longer guarantee.' To this objection you reply: 'If I understand you correctly, Mr Hardy, except for a longer guarantee from our competitors, you are perfectly satisfied with our product, is that not so? Therefore, if I can guarantee that our firm will stand behind its product in any circumstance, you are ready to buy from us, are you not?' Of course, your company's policy about guarantees will have to be explained at this point.

6. Friendship or reciprocity

- 'I always buy from this good friend of mine' *or* 'I always buy from Mr Bates, who is also an excellent client of mine.' When an objection of this nature is made, it helps to remind your prospect that profits come from a better product, not from the salesperson. You must sell your product or service on the basis of price, quality, after-sales service, delivery, guarantee, expertise, etc. You can say, 'I know that it's nice to buy from friends – I do it too – but I would like to point out the advantages of dealing with an independent salesperson without influence and without obligation'.

When facing 'friendship' objections, the easiest technique is to try for a 'small sale'. Once you have your foot in the door, it is not too difficult to obtain larger orders.

7. Other objections

Always agree with any and all objections and then turn the objection to your advantage and *close the sale!*

Summary

1. The sale often starts with your prospect's objection.
2. Always try to discover the *true objection*.
3. Use the objection to close the sale.
4. Questions that you pose in response to objections can become your key closing questions: 'Do I understand you correctly?', 'Isn't that right?', 'Isn't that so?'
5. Sometimes ask to return to the objection at the end of the presentation. At that point, use the objection to close the sale.
6. Never play 'ping-pong' with prospects who make objections.
7. Do not sidestep an objection.
8. Always be keen and interested in your prospect's objections.

Chapter 26

Closing the No-Close Sale

We've already said a lot about bringing the sale to a successful conclusion. Posing a key question that leads to an affirmative answer is one good way of closing. You can also take the prospect's objections and turn them around to your advantage. But sometimes you will find – as I have – that this is not enough. If that happens, you might become discouraged. You discovered the prospect's wavelength, you cultivated empathy, but nothing happened. Don't give up! Keep on trying, but don't push too hard – just hard enough.

If you've really tried everything and your prospect is still showing no interest, you have one last closing method left. It helps in many cases. But try it only after all else has failed. Tell your prospect about Napoleon – Napoleon Bonaparte, the great French emperor, who ruled France and many other countries in the early nineteenth century.

The Napoleon system

When the Emperor had to make an important decision, he used a foolproof system: he would take a sheet of paper and draw a vertical dividing line down the middle. One side was for advantages and the other for disadvantages. He would list these and later add them up. The longest list would then automatically dictate his final decision.

'So, Mr Nichol,' you can say, 'to help you come up with the right decision, let us try the Napoleon system. Let us take this sheet of paper and list the "FORS" on this side and the "AGAINSTS" of my proposal on the other.'

FOR	AGAINST

Then hand your prospect your pen if he isn't holding one already.

You start by dictating all the advantages of your product. He *writes them down.* Take the opportunity to emphasize details if necessary. Say, 'Don't you think . . .', 'What about . . .' You let him list, *in his own handwriting*, about 20 or more advantages.

When he runs short of other ideas and you have run out of suggestions, you say, 'Now let's list the disadvantages of my product'. And here you *shut up! Don't say another word! You wait! Silently!*

In my many years of selling, I have never seen a prospect

list more than four items in the right-hand column. When he has finished, you close by *counting the 'fors'*: one, two . . . five . . . twenty . . . twenty-two . . . and once more *you wait!* No more talking until he says something. What can he say? Usually, 'Well, I see . . .'

Think of the psychological effect of this closing method: the prospect himself writes the advantages he would get from buying your product or service. Immediately afterwards he lists and counts the disadvantages of becoming your client. It's obvious that it is to his advantage to buy, wouldn't you say?

Once you have tried this system I know you will always use it! I know! I have seen thousands use it effectively.

Ask forgiveness!

The Napoleon system is really the second-last method you can use in a situation where you've tried everything else and not yet closed the sale. To conclude this chapter on a happy note, let me describe a funny closing method that some people use very effectively. I have never tried it myself, but I know a number of salespeople who like it!

You must admit that it is rare to hear a salesperson beg for forgiveness! But that is exactly what these professionals do. Here is how it has been described to me.

The method is used at the very end of a presentation. You have not closed, you have said goodbye and you're on the point of leaving. Suddenly, near the door, you turn around and take a few steps back, saying, 'Ms Rees, please forgive me. I am truly sorry! I have not been able to convince you. I sincerely hope that you will accept my apologies.'

As it is *very unusual* to hear a salesperson ask forgiveness, the prospect always says, 'Of course'. Furthermore, she is happy to be rid of you and glad to see you go, so she forgives easily!

Now you must take this opportunity to *ask for her help!* This is even more unusual! You say, 'Ms Rees, please help me! I do not want to make the same mistake again at my next appointment. Please tell my why I was not able to convince you to become my client. Was it the price? Was it the delivery arrangement? Was it my personality? Was it . . .? And you keep on asking until she gives you the true reason for not buying.

When she has given you the real reason for her refusal, you return to her desk, open your briefcase and say, 'Perhaps I didn't make myself totally clear before. Please let me show you again . . .' And you start a partial presentation, trying to close again, now that you know the real reason for her refusal.

I can see you smiling again. I agree with you – it is a funny way to reopen a lost presentation, but I am told it works! So if it works for some people, why not try it? You run no risk in doing so!

Never linger at the end of a sale

It is good professional practice to leave as soon as possible after closing a sale. Unless your new client insists that you stay, don't waste time waiting around. The most efficient way is to thank him and go.

It is logical and simple to go without delay. Your time is precious and so is his. Some professionals think that if the salesperson stays too long after closing a sale, the client may change his mind and reverse his decision.

When you are ready to go, you can say, 'I know you'll be happy with your decision, Mr London. I'll be on my way now. I have to take care of the paperwork so that your machine will be delivered as soon as possible. Thank you again.' By leaving in this way, you are showing courtesy and professionalism.

Other salespeople, when taking their leave, mention that they have to get on to their next appointment. This, too, should be done courteously, to ensure that the new client does not feel less important than the next prospect.

Summary

1. If all else fails, use the Napoleon system to help your prospect make a decision.
2. By asking for forgiveness at the end of an unsuccessful presentation, you get another chance to reopen the presentation.
3. After a close, do not linger.
4. Thank your client sincerely, and congratulate her on her decision.

Chapter 27

Always Ask for Referrals

The salesperson's most important list is the list of prospective clients. Anyone in our business who finds a 'mine' of prospects is on the road to riches. For newcomers, finding prospects is one of *the* major difficulties. I would even venture to say that 90 per cent of new salespeople and trainees do not realise the importance of this facet of our profession.

Friends

Most people go through life with a few good friends and many acquaintances. Without them, life would seem dull. For the salesperson, a client's circle of friends is also an excellent source of prospects.

When I buy a new car, I rapidly become an 'assistant' to the salesperson who sold it to me. If he is a pro, he will take advantage of my satisfaction as a new owner. I could send him acquaintances, friends and neighbours. He has learned how to ask! You can too!

Some salespeople never hesitate to say to their referrals. 'Your friend, Mr Pearson, has asked me to come and see you . . .' I have never liked this approach and have often found that an opening of this nature leads the prospect to believe that his friend wanted to get rid of the salesperson. In order to do so gently, he sent the salesperson to the new prospect.

I have always preferred to make appointments without mentioning the friend's name. Later, somewhere in the middle of the presentation, I bring up his or her name. After having broken the ice, at some point I would say, 'By the way, Mr Pearson, who I believe you know, mentioned your name in very friendly terms. He is a good client of mine.' This little remark could be of great help if you use it well.

The endless chain

If you are able to create an 'endless chain' of new prospects, you will never be without an appointment. I know a good salesman who makes a game of it. He starts with an original list of 50 prospects. Every time he makes a sale he replaces that prospect's name with a new one. His technique is a good one! After completing the sale, he tells his newly acquired client, 'Mr Matthews, I am delighted to have you as a client. However, I am now facing a dilemma. I have just lost a prospect. Would you help me to replace yourself on my list of prospects with a good friend, relation or colleague who may be in need of my services?' Using such a simple request, this pro always keeps his list of prospects at 50 and sometimes the list even grows!

Asking for referrals from no-sale prospects

Should you request referrals from prospects to whom you were unable to sell? There are two schools of thought on this subject. Some people will say that it is unsafe to request referrals from unsold prospects. You could face the question, 'Why should I buy if my friend didn't buy from you?'

Others will say that it is easier to obtain good referrals from unsold prospects because someone you have spent an hour with *unsuccessfully* will feel in some way obliged to do something for you. She will *gladly* give you one or two good referrals.

It is also known that most salespeople have more unsold prospects than clients. Remember: the best of us can sell to only one out of every three prospects. Therefore, if each unsold prospect gives you only *one* referral, you will have an ever-increasing list of prospects. This is why I do not hesitate to ask unsold prospects for referrals.

When should you ask for referrals?

If you sell services or products requiring after-sales servicing or return visits, I suggest that you ask for referrals only when you come back for the second time. Your new client will be much more relaxed and satisfied. He or she will never refuse to give you someone else's name.

If, on the other hand, your product is to be delivered by others or if it requires installation by a professional crew, it is best to request referrals at the end of the sale.

How do you ask for referrals?

Here again everything depends on the product sold. Selling financial services or life insurance requires more diplomacy than selling vacuum cleaners, cars or encyclopedias when it comes to asking for referrals. Your new financial client could think that you are going to talk to her friends or relations about her own investments. For this reason, she might be more reluctant to give names than a car salesperson's client would be.

It is not enough to ask for 'names of prospective clients'.

It is better to ask your new client if he would like to *help* a relation or friend by letting you introduce your services or product to him. Few people refuse to help others if they are asked to do so.

At the end of the sale or visit, say, 'Mr Blessington, there is surely someone close to you that you would like to help . . . Of course, it's understood that I will not mention your name if you would prefer I didn't.'

Let's take the example of Mr Jones, who gives you the name of his nephew Smith, but asks you not to reveal his name. How is that done? It's easy. This is what you say to Mr Smith when you see him:

'One of your good friends has suggested I come to see you.'

'Who would that be?' Smith asks.

'If I may, Mr Smith, I'll answer your question in a few minutes.'

At the end of your sale or presentation to Mr Smith, you will also ask for referrals. At that time you will also add, 'Earlier, Mr Smith, you asked who sent me to see you. I was told not to mention your friend's name and I did not! Should you make the same request for friends or family, you can also be assured of my discretion. I will not reveal your name. I'm sure you understand, Mr Smith.'

This is a very professional way of selling. Everyone you talk to in these terms will be impressed. No one will continue to ask you for the name of the person who sent you to them! And they will be happy to give you referrals. In fact, you will have more referrals than time to see them all.

In other circumstances, this method is used: 'Mr Jones, I will not reveal to Mr Smith that you have suggested I see him. But I am sure you would have no objection to my saying that you and I know each other.'

It has been proved the world over that the best source of new business is a newly acquired client. This holds true for all services and products. After buying a new car I feel like a sub-dealer. Because of my enthusiasm for the car I have just purchased, I become an excellent spokesman for my dealer to my neighbours, friends and relatives.

Think of it! Your new clients are happy and proud of their acquisition. They will be eager to talk about it and will even boast about it! They will be your best publicity agents!

Remember, your return visit is important, even if it is only a friendly call and not a mandatory after-sales service. By returning to see your clients and making a habit of it, you will acquire new names and have a never-ending chain of prospects.

Summary

1. The salesperson's most important list is the list of prospective clients.
2. Friends of newly acquired clients are the best prospects.
3. Create your own endless chain of prospects.
4. You can also ask for referrals from unsold prospects. Your time will not be wasted!
5. In many cases, it is easier to obtain referrals on second calls.
6. Ask your clients to *help* their friends and relatives by letting you present the advantages of your services or products.
7. Never reveal the name of someone who wants to remain anonymous.
8. Always ask for referrals.

Chapter 28

Should You Go Back?

In my earliest days as a salesman, a friend referred me to his business partner. At the end of my presentation, this prospect asked me to come back the next Wednesday because, although he was in a hurry, he did want to invest with me.

As requested, I went back to see him on Wednesday and also on *seven* additional occasions! The man never bought! It made me discover that there are people in this world who cannot say no. It was a good lesson! Since then, I have never gone back to see anyone more than twice after my first presentation.

You must learn to evaluate your prospective clients, depending on your product. Never miss an opportunity to make a sale, but never waste your valuable time with people who are afraid of saying no.

Experience has also taught me that there are few people who really do 'think about' any purchase proposal between your first presentation and your next appointment. Usually, by asking you to come back later, they are just using an excuse! As soon as you are outside their door, they go back to their routine and *do not think about your product or service again.*

You might have noticed already (if not, you will!) how 'cold' prospects become between appointments. Sometimes they even completely forget the interesting explanations you have given them on your first visit. To call a second time is therefore always more difficult, and usually requires more tact!

On your first visit, there was an element of novelty and curiosity. On your return call, these elements are no longer there to assist you. You are now at a disadvantage: your face and personality are now known to your prospect. You must act with even more tact and subtlety to close sales on second and third calls! Your *savoir-faire* and empathy will be tested!

What to do on a second call

My first word of advice is to take along something new. You could take new drawings, tests, diagrams, articles, pictures, samples or surveys. And you could phrase your proposal differently. You have to show your prospect that you have been working on her case and have her interests at heart. In short, you have to think of something that would make your product even more interesting the second time around.

My second word of advice is to use the element of surprise. Go back to your prospect without an appointment. Your first words will be crucial. You *cannot* afford to let him say, 'I'm not interested', before you have a chance to say anything. I usually like to start with a résumé of the advantages of my product – this leads me to my closing attempt.

What you must not do!

How many times have I heard a trainee say on the second call: 'Did you get a chance, Ms Leeson, to think about my proposal?' or perhaps, 'You remember my first visit, Mr Wakefield, don't you? Have you had a chance to think about my presentation?' Questions like these are absolutely *taboo* in our profession! They automatically open the door to *negative* answers. You must *never* ask them.

Be *positive*. Don't ask questions! Assume that your prospect is going to buy today! Believe it! To the very end, you must have faith in your ability to close your sale *today*! Don't ever give your prospect the opportunity to answer no by asking a question. Isn't it easier to say, 'Mr Andrews, I have returned today to open your account'?

Never return empty-handed. Always carry that little item that will renew your prospect's interest and let you close the sale. Do so with dignity, assurance and your best *smile*. Reflect your optimism and always show respect. Be courteous and helpful to the very end.

Summary

1. Learn to identify prospects who can't say no.
2. Generally, it's a waste of time to see a prospect more than three times.
3. All second interviews put the salesperson at a disadvantage.
4. Few prospects, if any, 'think about' buying between the first and second visits.
5. Always take something new with you – samples or information – on a second visit.
6. A 'surprise' second visit can give you a slight edge.
7. On a surprise visit, never let the prospect say 'No thanks' before you've said anything.
8. On a return appointment, never ask a question like 'Have you thought about it?'
9. On the second visit, reflect optimism and confidence, and show courtesy with a smile.

Conclusion

This is not the end! Selling is a continual learning process. Since this book was first published, I have learned much myself. Some readers have told me about new selling methods; others have written to tell me their personal experiences. The reward for writing a manual like this (ego trip aside!) is that you usually receive praise and criticism. I welcome both!

Some of you will find ways of using my tips and suggestions to improve your business and your daily lives. Your success will be sweet music to my ears! For various reasons, others will have criticisms to make. Their comments will help me to improve and search further.

For the rest of this extraordinary century, those who are willing to work hard and make personal sacrifices will successfully reach new goals. Never look back! Get ready to step into the twenty-first century with enthusiasm and the desire to learn and improve yourself!

Further Reading from Kogan Page

Denny, Richard. *Selling to Win; Tested Techniques for Closing the Sale*. 1989.

Ley D Forbes. *The Best Seller*. 1988.

Mercer, David. *The Sales Professional: Strategies and Techniques for Managing the High-level Sale*. 1988.

Rogers, Len. *Selling by Telephone: Tested Techniques to Make Every Call Count*. 1986.

Schiffman, Stephan. *Cold Calling Techniques*. 1989.

Schiffman, Stephan. *The 25 Most Common Sales Mistakes . . . and How to Avoid Them*. 1991.

Tirbutt, Edmund. *How to Increase Sales Without Leaving Your Desk*. 1991.